Essential Series

Springer

London
Berlin
Heidelberg
New York
Barcelona
Hong Kong
Milan
Paris
Santa Clara
Singapore
Tokyo

Also in this series:

John Cowell
Essential Visual Basic 4.0 *fast*
3-540-19998-5

John Cowell
Essential Delphi 2.0 *fast*
3-540-76026-1

John Cowell
Essential Java *fast*
3-540-76052-0

John Cowell
Essential Visual Basic 5.0 *fast*
3-540-76148-9

Duncan Reed and Peter Thomas
Essential HTML *fast*
3-540-76199-3

John Cowell
Essential Delphi 3 *fast*
3-540-76150-0

John Hunt
Essential JavaBeans *fast*
1-85233-032-5

John Vince
Essential Virtual Reality *fast*
1-85233-012-0

John Cowell
Essential Visual J++ 6.0 *fast*
1-85233-013-9

John Cowell
Essential Java 2 *fast*
1-85233-071-6

John Cowell

Essential
Visual Basic 6.0
fast

 Springer

John Cowell, BSc (Hons), MPhil., PhD.
Department of Computer and Information Sciences, De Montfort University,
Kents Hill Campus, Hammerwood Gate, Kents Hill,
Milton Keynes MK7 6HP, UK

ISBN 1-85233-207-7 Springer-Verlag London Berlin Heidelberg

British Library Cataloguing in Publication Data
Cowell, John, 1957-
    Essential Visual Basic 6.0 fast
    1.Visual Basic (Computer program language) 2.Visual
    programming (Computer science)
    I.Title II.Visual Basic 6.0 fast
    005.1'33
    ISBN 1852332077

Library of Congress Cataloging-in-Publication Data
A catalog record for this book is available from the Library of Congress

Typesetting: Camera-ready by author
Printed and bound by Creative Print & Design Group (Wales), Ebbw Vale
34/3830-543210 Printed on acid-free paper SPIN 10741535

Contents

1
Why Use Visual Basic 6.0?

Introduction

Visual Basic is a part of the Microsoft Visual Studio and is the flagship development language for Microsoft. You can develop applications for a stand–alone or networked computer system, you can create your own controls and even develop applications for the Internet. Visual Basic is closely integrated with Microsoft's database tools, in fact virtually any application you wish to create can be produced in Visual Basic.

The flexibility of Visual Basic is one reason for its success, another is that the language is straightforward to use, with a much less difficult syntax than most other languages.

The Visual Basic Integrated Development Environment (IDE) is now very similar to other Microsoft IDEs such as Visual C++ and Visual J++. It is an excellent user interface, which is flexible, and because all its features operate in a consistent way it will quickly seem familiar and easy to use.

If you want to develop applications in a Windows environment, Visual Basic 6.0 is probably the best development available. The aim of this book is to help you to develop applications in Visual Basic 6.0 fast.

Visual Basic 6.0 editions

Microsoft have produced three different versions of Visual Basic 6.0:

- The Learning edition is suitable for small–scale developments. It has all the intrinsic controls and a number of additional controls such as the grid and data–bound controls. The documentation includes the *Learn VB Now* and the Microsoft (MSDN) CD. Most students would find this edition suitable.
- The Professional edition has many additional ActiveX controls, integrated database development tools, the DHTML Page Designer, and the Internet

Information Server Application Designer. Additional documentation is provided to cover these additional features. This edition is intended for the majority of professional developers.

- The Enterprise edition is designed for developers working in a team environment. It includes the Back Office tools such as SQL Server, Microsoft Transaction Server, Internet Information Server, Visual SourceSafe and numerous other tools.

All examples in this book were tested using the Professional edition, but virtually all of them could have been written in the Learning edition. The Windows 98 operating system was used.

What computer do you need to run Visual Basic 6.0?

Computers are never fast enough, and so the faster your computer the better. If you are a professional developer or the cost of your computer is not an issue you will obtain excellent performance with:

- Intel Pentium III 500.
- 128Mb of memory.
- 17" monitor.

Realistically, though Visual Basic is not particularly demanding in its hardware requirements and reasonable performance for smaller applications can be obtained with a much slower machine with less memory. The minimum specification for reasonable performance is:

- Intel Pentium 150.
- 32MB or more of memory.
- 15" monitor.

If your computer is slower or has less memory than this you can still use it: you will just have to be more patient.

A CD drive is also needed for installation of the software. If disk space is a problem you can install a minimal version of the MSDN documentation on the hard disk which will refer to the MSDN CD which you must place in the CD drive. It is better if you have the space to install all of the MSDN documentation on your hard disk so that it can be accessed much faster.

The Visual Basic 6.0 development environment requires you to have at least four or five windows open at the same time. Ideally you will need an SVGA screen, and even if you have excellent eyesight a monitor of 15 inches or more is a great help.

Why change to version 6.0?

There are some significant changes to this version of Visual Basic which make it worthwhile changing if you are using an earlier version. The major changes include:

- Improved database development tools, in particular the ADO data control.
- Numerous new controls including the DateTimePicker, the CoolBar control, the MonthView control and many others.
- Improved facilities in the creation of ActiveX components.
- New language features.
- Extended Internet capabilities.

In addition to some major new facilities, version 6.0 of Visual Basic has numerous small improvements in the user interface, and it has the family look of Visual J++ and Visual C++ which are two other parts of the Microsoft Visual Studio. If you become familiar with the Visual Basic 6.0 environment it will be a big help if you want to use these other languages as well.

Is this book for you?

This books assumes that you are familiar with using Windows applications, such as spreadsheets and databases, but does not assume that you have any prior knowledge of using Visual Basic or a similar Integrated Development Environment (IDE): it is therefore suitable for the beginner. If you have some experience of programming, particularly in using an IDE, you will find that this book allows you to speed through the introductory material in the early chapters to the more complex aspects in the later chapters. If you want to learn how to develop applications in Visual Basic, but do not have time to read a 1000–page book, you will find that *Essential Visual Basic 6.0 Fast* is an excellent way to learn how to develop applications in Visual Basic quickly.

Visual Basic has an excellent Help system which is supplied on the MSDN CD, which also contains the Help system for Visual J++ and Visual C++. There are the usual search facilities, which are fine if you know Visual Basic well and are familiar with the terminology and concepts; what the Help system does not provide is a readable, impartial guide to the language and environment. This book does not cover every minor detail of Visual Basic in the same way as the Help system, but it does give you a grasp of all the most important features of the language. There are many illustrations and examples. The best way to learn Visual Basic is to try out the examples for yourself.

How to use this book

This book contains many examples to illustrate the ideas it covers; you can read through from the beginning to the end, but where possible each chapter has been written to be self contained, so that if, for example, you want to find out how to create a menu system you can just read that chapter without the need to read the preceding chapters.

If you are unfamiliar with Visual Basic you should start at the beginning and work through the first six chapters which deal with the basics of the Visual Basic IDE and language.

Chapters 7 to 11 cover additional aspects of Visual Basic including using menus, dialogs and forms, ActiveX controls, mouse and keyboard events and how to create and use procedures and functions.

Chapter 12 deals with creating and using classes and objects. Visual Basic is not an object–oriented language but it does have some object–oriented features.

Chapter 13 covers debugging. As the applications you develop become more complex you will need to use the excellent debugging facilities of Visual Basic to find and fix bugs.

Chapters 14 to 17 cover the development of database applications. Particular importance has been given to this area since virtually all real–world applications use databases.

Chapter 18 shows how you can create ActiveX documents, which are Visual Basic applications with may contain hypertext links and are run within a container such as an Internet browser.

This book does not cover every aspect of Visual Basic: if it did it would be ten times its size and take much longer to read. What this book does is focus on the most widely used features of Visual Basic that you need to start to develop Visual Basic applications *fast*.

Conventions

There are a few conventions used in this book which make it easier to read:

- All program examples are in *italics.*
- All reserved words such as **For**..**Next** are in **bold** and start with a capital.
- Menu options are shown in **bold**, for example, **File | Print** which means the **Print** option from the **File** menu.
- All user created identifiers such as *MyFile* are in italics.

2

The Visual Basic IDE

Introduction

Visual Basic 6.0 is the latest version of one of the most widely–used development environments in the world. It has an extensive range of facilities. You can create Windows applications, DLLs, ActiveX controls, Web–based applications and powerful database systems. The only negative aspect of this flexibility is that if you are new to Visual Basic the range of options available can seem overwhelming. It is very important in the early stages not to panic when you see the Visual Basic Integrated Development Environment (IDE). It is one of the best development environments available and you will find that after a few hours it will look familiar. In this chapter we are going to look at the key aspects of the IDE. In particular we are going to look at:

- The design form.
- The Project Explorer.
- The Toolbox.
- The Form Layout window.
- The Properties window.
- The tool bar.
- The menu bar.

Running Visual Basic

When you have installed Visual Basic 6.0 on your computer you can run it by clicking on the **Start** button and selecting the **Programs | Microsoft Visual Basic 6.0 | Microsoft Visual Basic 6.0** option.

If you are using Windows 98, or a recent version of Windows 95, and want to create a shortcut and place it on your desktop, right click on **Microsoft Visual Basic 6.0** as shown in figure 2.1 and select the **Create Shortcut** option from the speed menu. The shortcut you have created can be dragged from this menu system to your desktop. Visual Basic can then be run by double clicking on this shortcut.

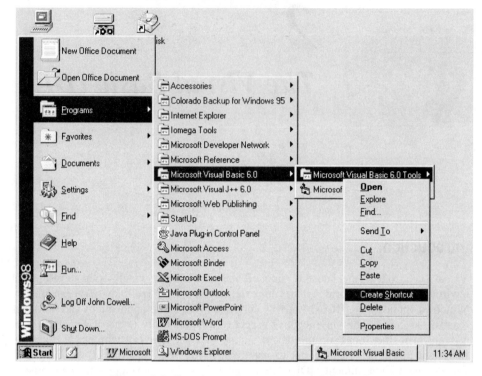

Figure 2.1 *Creating a shortcut to Visual Basic 6.0.*

All of the files in a Visual Basic application are contained within a project. When you start to create an application you need to create a new project. To continue work on an existing application you must open its project file. When you run Visual Basic, you will see the window shown in figure 2.2. This window has three pages which can be displayed by choosing one of the three tabs.

- The **New** tab (shown in figure 2.2) is used to start a new project.
- The **Existing** tab allows you to browse through your file system and choose an existing project to open.
- The **Recent** tab is also used to open an existing project. Visual Basic keeps a record of the projects you have worked on recently and displays them on this page. You can select the project you want to open.

Visual Basic is able to create a wide variety of types of applications, such as ActiveX DLLs, ActiveX controls, and database applications. In addition there are a number of wizards which can be used to get your application off to a quick start. The first applications we are going to develop are **Standard EXE** applications which produce Windows executable files, so you should select this option.

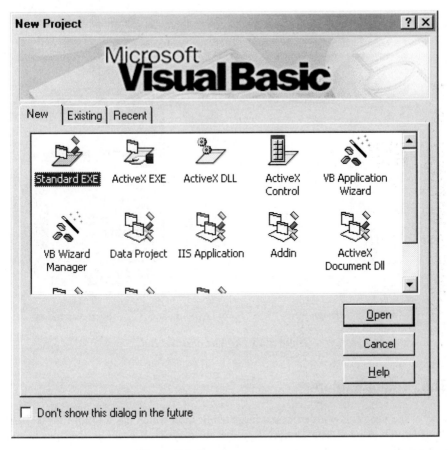

Figure 2.2 *Starting a new project.*

If you choose to open an existing project, all of the files in that project are available for you to view or change within the IDE. If you start a new application, a new empty project is created as shown in figure 2.3.

The IDE has the following components which we are going to look at:

- The Project Explorer.
- The design form.
- The Toolbox.
- The Properties window.
- The Form Layout window.
- The menu bar.
- The tool bar.

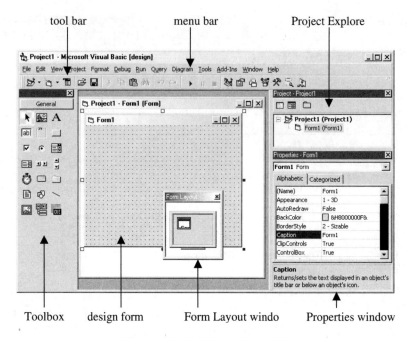

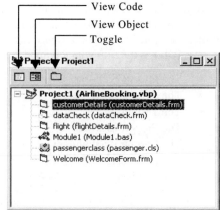

Figure 2.3 The Visual Basic IDE.

The Project Explorer

One of the problems with writing a large application which has a lot of files is finding the file you want. The Project Explorer displays a list of all the files in your application.

Figure 2.4 The Project Explorer.

You can display a file by selecting it in this window. There are two different ways in which this window shows the components of your project, both shown in figure 2.4.

The view on the left lists the files in categories, which can make a file easier to find. You can also choose to expand or compress a list of files in a category by using the + and – icons adjacent to the category titles.

The view on the right simply lists all of the files in the project.

In both views the name of the form or module is given first, followed by the name of the file in which it exists. You can switch between these views by clicking on the toggle icon.

In Visual Basic every form has some Basic code associated with it which responds to events which happen on the form, for example clicking on a button or selecting an item from a list. The **View Object** and **View Code** icons allow you to switch between the form and this background code. If you select a component such as a class module which does not have a form connected with it, the **View Object** icon is disabled.

The design form

Most applications in Visual Basic have at least one window or form which may display information or accept input. To display a particular form, select it from the Project Explorer and click on the **View Object** icon.

You can change the size of a form by dragging one of the black squares as shown in figure 2.5. The size of the form at design–time is the same as its size when the application runs, although you can resize a form at run –time by writing some Visual Basic instructions or by dragging one of the edges of the form in the usual way.

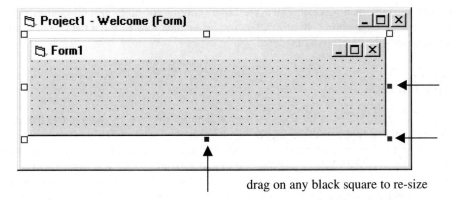

drag on any black square to re-size

Figure 2.5 The design form.

By default there is a grid of dots over the form; when you add controls such as buttons and labels to the form they automatically snap to the nearest grid dot and adjust their size so that their width and height correspond to an integer number of grid dots. This is a useful feature since it helps you to line up your components and give a professional look to your applications. You can vary the distance between the grid dots, or even switch off the snap facility altogether by using the **Tools | Options** menu option and selecting the **General** tab as shown in figure 2.6.

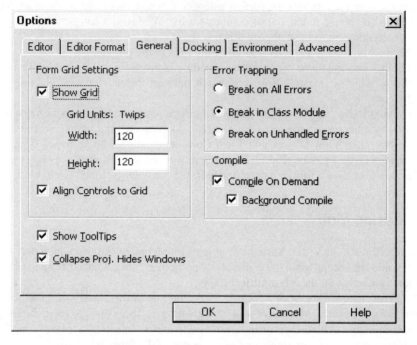

Figure 2.6 Changing the grid settings.

The **Format** menu has an extensive set of options for aligning and controlling the spacing of components. If an application is to look professional the layout of the controls must be carefully considered.

The Toolbox

If you want to add a control to a form you must first select that control from the Toolbox. Then move to the design form and drag the mouse. The position where you first press the left mouse button when you start dragging is anchored and becomes one of the corners of the control. If you want to add another control you must select it from the Toolbox and repeat the process. If you want to add more than one control of the same type press the **Ctrl** button while selecting the control you wish to add from the Toolbox. You can now add as many controls of that type as you wish without having to reselect the control each time.

The Visual Basic Toolbox may contain two types of controls:

- Intrinsic controls. These are basic controls which the Toolbox will always contain and are an integral part of the Visual Basic IDE. They cannot be deleted.

- ActiveX controls. These controls can be added or deleted from the Toolbox, they are stored as separate files which have an OCX extension. Versions 4.0 and earlier of Visual Basic use files with a VBX extension. Where possible Visual Basic 6.0 will automatically replace a VBX file in an application with the equivalent OCX file.

Figure 2.7 shows two different forms of the Toolbox. The Toolbox on the left shows only the intrinsic controls; the Toolbox on the right also has numerous ActiveX controls.

Figure 2.7 *The Toolbox.*

We look at the intrinsic controls in the next chapter and at some of the ActiveX controls in later chapters.

Adding ActiveX controls

For simple Windows applications, which do not use ActiveX technology, or connect to the Web, or need access to a remote database, the intrinsic controls may be sufficient. However one of the reasons why Visual Basic is such a good development tool is that there is a very wide range of OCX files available. Some have been written by Microsoft, but the majority have been written by other software companies. If you are starting to write a new application it is worthwhile checking to see if you can buy some additional controls which will save you rewriting code which you can buy cheaply. If you cannot find the control you want, Visual Basic allows you to create your own ActiveX controls.

If you want to add a new control to your Toolbox choose the **Project | Components** menu option, shown in figure 2.8, and choose the control you wish to add. It will automatically appear on Toolbox.

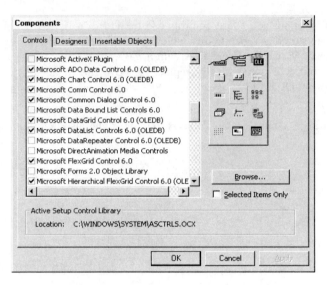

Figure 2.8 Adding ActiveX controls.

The Properties window

Figure 2.9 The Properties window.

Every control in your application has a set of properties which control the position of the control, its size, the font it uses to display text and so on. If you select a control, its properties are displayed in the Properties window. This window has two alternative views as shown in figure 2.9. You can display the properties in alphabetical order or grouped into categories. If you select a property, a brief description of that property is displayed at the bottom of the Properties window.

The Form Layout window

The Form Layout window allows you to specify visually where your forms will appear on the screen when the application is run. There is sometimes a problem if an application is run on a screen which has a different resolution to that on which the application is developed. If you right click on the Form Layout window and select the **Resolution Guides** option from the speed menu, you will see how the positioning of your window will be affected by different screen resolutions. Figure 2.10 was produced on a monitor with a resolution of 1024×768: the dotted lines on the figure show how it would appear on screens with a lower resolution.

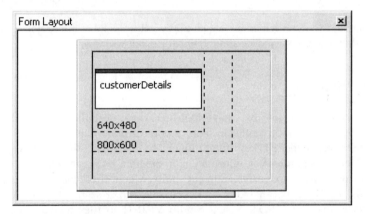

Figure 2.10 The Form Layout window.

All the forms which are open in your project will be displayed in the Form Layout window, you can move any of them by dragging. You cannot change the size of a window in the Form Layout window: to do this you must open that window and drag on one of the square blocks at its edge.

The menu bar and the tool bar

The menu bar provides access to all of the facilities of the Visual Basic environment. The tool bar provides a set of icons which allow you to access the most commonly–used options from the menu bar quickly. When you run Visual Basic for the first time only the standard tool bar is displayed. There are three others and you can display or hide any combination of them by using the **View | Tool bars** menu option and selecting **Debug**, **Edit**, **Form Editor** or **Standard**.

If you are not sure what a menu item does, you move the mouse to that item and wait for a few seconds until a tool tip is displayed which describes the item's function.

Finding elements of the IDE

One of the most annoying aspects of using an IDE as powerful as Visual Basic 6.0 is that there are so many different parts to it and it is easy to lose one of the windows you need, such as the Toolbox or the Properties window. Fortunately there are some straightforward ways of finding these key windows:

- The Project Explorer. Select the **View | Project Explorer** menu option or press **Ctrl+R.**
- The design form. Double click on the form you want to see in the Project Explorer.
- The Toolbox. Select the **View | Toolbox** menu option.
- The Properties window. Select the **View | Properties Window** menu option or press **F4**.
- The Form Layout window. Select the **View | Form Layout Window** menu option.

The standard tool bar has icons which allow you to display the Project Explorer, the Toolbox, the Properties window and the Form Layout window.

Getting Help

All of the items in the tool bars have tool tips which describe the icon. If you need more detailed information about an icon, a control or any other aspect of the visual environment: press the **F1** key after moving to that item: this displays a context–sensitive Help which gives you information on the item you have selected.

Visual Basic has an extensive Help capability which offers the usual facilities of an ordered list of contents, an index of key words and a search facility. One of the drawbacks is that the MSDN Visual Studio V6.0 Help files include information on other packages in the Visual Studio, such as Visual C++ and Visual J++. If you are dealing exclusively with Visual Basic this can be confusing. You can restrict the Help so that only entries which relate specifically to Visual Basic are used. To do this, in the **Active Subset** list on the top left of the Help facility select the **Visual Basic Documentation** option.

When installing Visual Basic you can install all of the MSDN Visual Studio documentation on your hard disk which takes 1.3Gb. The Visual Basic Help documentation takes about 600Mb, but if you are short of space you can install a minimal subset which takes 60Mb. If you do not choose to install the full documentation set you need to keep the CD with the Help information in your CD drive, which does take longer to access than if the information is installed on your hard disk. If there is room on your disk it is best to install it fully. Frequent updates are available from Microsoft which can easily be installed.

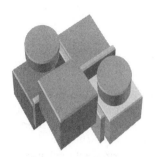

3
The Intrinsic Controls

Introduction

Most of the controls in the standard Toolbox will be familiar to anyone who has used a Windows application. In this chapter we are going to look at how you can use the standard controls in the Toolbox to create professional looking user interfaces.

Adding controls to a window

When you run Visual Basic the New Project window will prompt you to select the type of application you want to create. Select the **Standard EXE** option to create a stand–alone Windows executable application. If you are already running Visual Basic start a new project by selecting the **File | New Project** menu option to see the New Project window.

This application will automatically have one window, which will be displayed when you run the application. Its position on the screen can be controlled by the Form Layout window. We will see in chapter 8 how to add additional windows to your application and how to switch between windows.

In the Toolbox all of the icons except for one represent different controls. The arrow in the top left corner of the Toolbox, shown in figure 3.1, is used to select any controls you have placed on a window.

Figure 3.1 *The Selection tool.*

To add a control to a window, select the control in the Toolbox and then move to the window where you want to add the control. Drag the mouse to draw the control: the position where you start to drag will become one corner of the control. Do not worry if the control is not in the correct position or is the wrong size it is easy to change these things at any time. By default the control will be aligned to the grid squares which are shown on the window.

Selecting, moving and resizing controls

When you have added a control to a form, the selection tool is automatically selected in the Toolbox. If you want to add another control of the same type you must select that control again in the Toolbox and repeat the process. If you wish to add several controls of the same type you can press the **Ctrl** button as you select the control you want to add from the Toolbox. The type of control you choose in the Toolbox remains selected until you explicitly select another control type.

To select a control you have placed on a form, click on it. If you want to change the size of the control, select it by clicking on it and then dragging one of the handles as shown in figure 3.2.

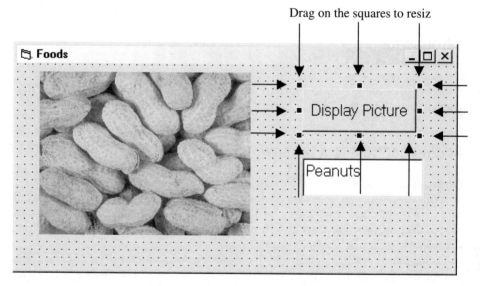

Figure 3.2 Selecting, resizing and moving controls.

You can move a control by dragging it. If you press the mouse on a control before moving it, the co–ordinates of the top left corner are displayed adjacent to the mouse pointer. If the co–ordinates are displayed they change as you move the control to reflect its new position.

You can select more than one control in two ways:

- If you press the **Ctrl** key at the same time as you select a control, any controls which have already been selected are not deselected.
- If you drag the mouse from a point outside of any control, a dotted rectangle appears; any control which is wholly or partly in that rectangle when the mouse button is released is selected.

All of the selected controls can be dragged together, so that they retain their relative positions, by pressing the mouse on one of the selected controls and dragging.

The Label control

The simplest of the controls in the standard Toolbox is the Label control, shown in figure 3.3.

     Figure 3.3 The Label control.

This control is usually used to display text which does not change while the application is running, although if you wish you can use a Label control to display a status message indicating the progress of a lengthy activity. The first Label you add to a window will have the default text *Label1*, the second *Label2* and so on. If you want to change this text you have to use the Properties window to alter the **Caption** property.

Changing the properties of a control

Every control has a set of properties. The value of these properties determines every aspect of the control's behaviour. Some properties can only be changed at run–time, that is when the application is executing, but the majority can be changed at both run–time and design–time. To change the properties of a control, select it. Its properties are displayed in the Properties window. If you cannot see the Properties window select the **View | Properties Window** menu option or press **F4**.

The type of the control and its name are displayed in a TextBox at the top of the Properties window.

To change a property of a control, select the control and click on that property in the Properties window. There are three different ways of changing property values:

- Typing the value of the new property. The **Caption** property, for example, contains the text which is displayed in a Label control. Whatever text you type automatically appears in the Label.
- Some properties have a button with three dots adjacent to the property value; clicking on this button displays a dialog. The **Font** property is an example of this type. Clicking on this button displays the Font dialog as shown in figure 3.4. Select the property values you want from the dialog and press the **OK** button.
- Some properties have a few options which are displayed in a list so that you can select the value you want. The **BackColor** property is an example of this type of property as shown in figure 3.5. Clicking on the down arrow displays the menu (which may be a selection of colour or text) and you can choose the value that you want for this property.

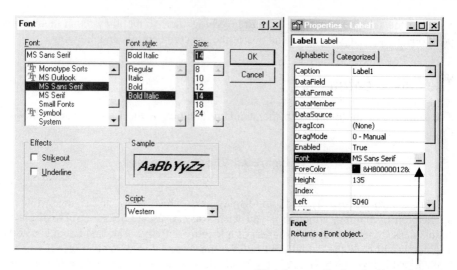

Click here to display the Font dialog

*Figure 3.4 Changing the **Font** property.*

Click here to display the list of colours

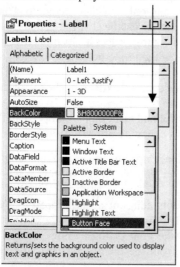

*Figure 3.5 Changing the **BackColor** property.*

Common properties

One of the major concerns for programmers who are unused to using a Windows IDE is that there are so many properties for the controls. Fortunately many of the properties are common to many controls and are used in the same way. Most applications require a small set of the available properties which you will quickly learn.

The following properties are common to most of the controls which are visible at run–time:

- The **Name** property is used by Visual Basic to uniquely identify each control. If you want you can rely on the default names created by Visual Basic, for example *Label1*, *Label2* and so on, but for serious applications it is usually best to give controls your own meaningful names.
- The **Height** and **Width** determine the size of the control.
- The **Top** and **Left** determine the distance of the top left corner of the control from the top left corner of the window on which it is displayed.
- If the **Enabled** property is **True** the control is available for use at run–time. If it is **False** it is disabled and appears "greyed out".
- The **Visible** property is **True** if the control can be seen. An invisible control is also disabled.
- The **ToolTipText** property allows you to provide some help at run–time. If the mouse rests over a control the text assigned to the **ToolTipText** property is displayed.
- The **Font** property determines the type and size of the font used to display text.
- The **BackColor** property gives the colour of the background of the control.
- The **Caption** property is used in a slightly different way in controls: for example it gives the text in a Label, the text on the face of a CommandButton control, the text adjacent to a CheckBox control and the text on the title bar of a window.

Some controls such as the Timer control, which informs your application when a specified amount of time has elapsed, are not visible at run–time and consequently have a very restricted (but adequate) set of properties.

Properties of the Label control

Apart from the properties which the Label control has in common with most other controls, the most often used properties are the **AutoSize** and **WordWrap** properties. These interact with each other to control the size of the label when the text specified in the **Caption** property is too large to be displayed in the Label at its current size.

If the **AutoSize** property is **True** and the **WordWrap** property is also **True** the control expands vertically to fit the text (unless a single long word is typed which can only be fully seen if the Label expands horizontally). If the **WordWrap** property is **False**, the label expands horizontally to fit the text.

If the **AutoSize** property is **False**, the control remains the same size and automatically wraps on to the next line when a line is full, irrespective of the value of the **WordWrap** property. Some of the text may not be visible.

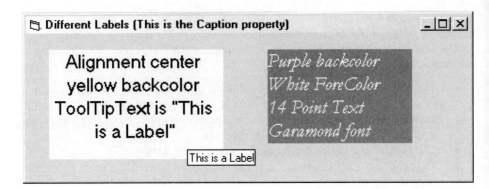

Figure 3.6 The Label control.

Figure 3.6 shows a running application with two Labels; the application does not do anything productive, but you can minimise and maximise the window and close the application by clicking on the three icons on the top right of the application. When the mouse lingers over the left Label, the **ToolTipText** is displayed.

If you are new to Visual Basic it is worthwhile taking the time to create the application shown in figure 3.6. You will need to start a new project, add two Label controls to the form and set some of the properties of the Labels. When you have done this you need to run the application to confirm that you have set the **ToolTipText** property correctly.

Running an application

There are three ways to run an application in Visual Basic:

- Select the **Run I Start** menu option.
- Press **F5**.
- Click on the Start icon on the standard tool bar as shown in figure 3.7.

Figure 3.7 The Start icon.

You can stop your application running in exactly the same way you would stop any other Windows application, by clicking on the close icon in the top right corner of the window.

The TextBox control

The TextBox control, shown in figure 3.8, can be used to display text in a manner similar to the Label control. The key difference is that a text can be typed into a TextBox and edited at run–time.

[abl]

Figure 3.8 *The TextBox control.*

The TextBox control does not have a **Caption** property. The text it displays is represented by the **Text** property. If you wish to display one than one line of text you must change the **MultiLine** property to **True** (the default is **False**). When you type more than one line of text, lines are terminated by **Ctrl+Return**. If the **MultiLine** property is **True** you can use the **Alignment** property to specify if the text is left justified, right justified or centred; the default is left justified.

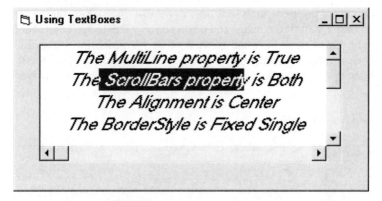

Figure 3.9 *The TextBox control.*

Figure 3.9 shows a TextBox control at run–time. You can type and delete text. You can also select text, but to cut and paste selected text requires some Visual Basic code to be written.

Passwords

You can use a TextBox control to type a password. If you set the **PasswordChar** property to any character, only the **PasswordChar** character appears when you run the application whatever text you try to type into that TextBox control. The usual character chosen is the asterisk * character. The text which is typed is available to your Visual Basic application as if it was displayed, and you can check to see if the text typed is a valid password. You can limit the length of the password typed using the **MaxLength** property.

The PictureBox and Image control

The PictureBox and Image controls, shown in figure 3.10, are used to display graphical images. The **Picture** property is used to specify the image. Most common format of graphics are supported: bitmap, icon, enhanced metafile, JPEG and GIF. The Image control uses fewer resources than a PictureBox, and can be displayed faster, but has reduced capabilities.

   Figure 3.10 *The PictureBox and Image control.*

You can not only display images in a PictureBox, you can also use it to display the output from the graphics methods (which can draw simple shapes such as rectangles and circles) and to display text produced by the **Print** method

Two properties in particular distinguish these two controls. The PictureBox control has the **AutoSize** property. When this is **True**, the control resizes itself to fit the image; the top left corner does not move. When it is **False**, the size of the control does not change and only a part of the image can be displayed. The Image control does not have this property, but it does have the **Stretch** property, which the PictureBox does not have. When the **Stretch** property is **True**, the image resizes itself to fit the Image control, when it is **False**, it does not and only a part of the image is displayed, as shown in figure 3.11.

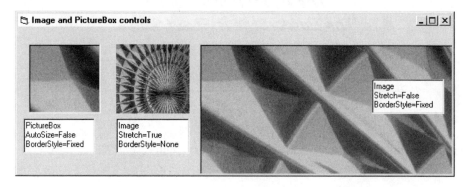

Figure 3.11 *The Image and PictureBox controls.*

The Image control has a default **BorderStyle** property of **None**, while for the PictureBox controls the default is **Fixed**. You can see the small difference that this makes in figure 3.11.

The CheckBox, OptionButton and Frame controls

We are going to look at these three controls (shown in figure 3.12) together, since they are often used with each other. The Frame control is used to group other controls together; it consists of a box with an optional title.

Figure 3.12 *The CheckBox, OptionButton and Frame controls.*

In figure 3.13, three Checkbox controls have been placed within a Frame. The **Caption** property of the Frame provides the Frame caption. The **Caption** property of the CheckBox controls provides the text adjacent to the CheckBox. If you create the Frame first and then add the CheckBox controls to it, the controls behave as a single unit and when you select and move the Frame all of the controls it contains are also moved. You can still move the Checkbox controls individually if you wish. If you create the Frame after the CheckBox controls, the visual appearance is the same, but you cannot move the controls as a group.

At run–time the Frame does not have any impact on the way the CheckBox controls behave. When you click on the CheckBox its state changes to hide or reveal a tick in the box. A tick indicates that you have chosen that item.

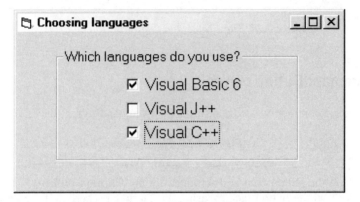

Figure 3.13 The Frame and CheckBox controls.

The **Value** property gives the state of the CheckBox: 0 indicates that the item is checked, 1 indicates that it is unchecked and 2 that the CheckBox item is unavailable. This property is not available at design–time and you will not see it listed in the Properties window. However, you can refer to it at run–time, but you need to write some Visual Basic code to do so.

The OptionButtons shown in figure 3.14 have the button on the right of the text since the **Alignment** property has been changed from the default **Left Justify** to **Right Justify**. These controls behave in a similar way to the CheckBox controls. The difference is that they are round rather than square and you can only select one of the controls within a group. When a new control in the group is selected all of the others are automatically deselected. If you add OptionButtons to a Frame they are grouped together and will behave as a unit. If you create the OptionButtons first and then add the Frame they will not be automatically grouped. If OptionButtons are not grouped with a container such as a Frame, the Form acts as a container.

CheckBox controls are used in situation, where you may select any number of options provided, OptionButtons are used when only one of the available options can be chosen.

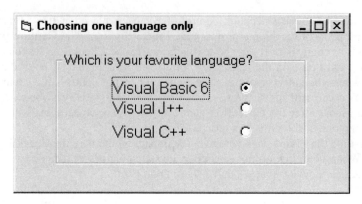

Figure 3.14 The Frame and OptionButton controls.

The CommandButton control

One of the most commonly–used controls is the CommandButton, shown in figure 3.15.

Figure 3.15 The CommandButton control.

The text on the button face is determined by the **Caption** property. You can also have a picture on the button face by using the **Picture** property. If the **DownPicture** property is not blank a different picture can be displayed when the button is pressed. The **DisabledPicture** property allows you to display a third picture if the button is disabled, that is if the **Enabled** property is **False**.

The **Cancel** property is useful: if this is set to **True**, pressing the **Escape** key anywhere on a form has the same affect as giving this CommandButton the focus and clicking it. Only one CommandButton on a form can have its **Cancel** property set to **True**.

4
Handling Events

Introduction

We have looked at some of the intrinsic controls in Visual Basic, but so far we have just used them to create attractive–looking user interfaces which do not do anything. All of the controls in Visual Basic not only have a set of properties, but also a set of events associated with them. When a button is clicked, or an item is selected from a list, an event occurs. If you want to take some action as a result of this type of event occurring you have to write some Visual Basic code. The Visual Basic IDE gives you a powerful but simple framework to respond to events. In this chapter we are going to look at the Visual Basic language and how to use it to write applications which are able to handle the Windows events which occur when your applications run.

Displaying pictures

The application we are going to develop is shown running in figure 4.1. If you click on one of the OptionButtons on the form on the left, a picture is displayed on the form on the right. The picture changes depending on which sport you select. If you want to choose some other picture file, click on the *Browse* OptionButton. This displays an open file dialog which allows you to search through the files on your system and select a picture file which is then displayed. If you want to print the picture click on the *Print* button. Clicking on the *Exit* button closes the application

To write an application such as this in many other environments would be a complex process, but it can be done in Visual Basic in a few minutes with a minimal amount of Visual Basic code.

Figure 4.1 *Displaying and printing pictures.*

Creating a new project

The first stage is to create a new project for this application:

- Select the **File | New Project** menu entry.
- Choose **Standard EXE** from the New Project Dialog displayed.
- Click the **OK** button.

This will create a stand–alone application which will run directly within a Windows environment.

Creating the user interface

The next stage is to create the input form where you specify what picture you want to display. Do not worry if initially the controls are not in exactly the correct position, or are the wrong size. It is easy to change this later.

If you cannot find any aspects of the environment, such as the Toolbox, use the **View** menu to specify the item you want to display, or the icons on the standard tool bar.

- Select the Frame icon on the Toolbox and draw the Frame on the form. The Frame icon is automatically deselected on the Toolbox.
- Select the OptionButton icon on the Toolbox while you are pressing the **Ctrl** button and add the first OptionButton to the Frame. This prevents the automatic de–selection of the OptionButton control on the Toolbox and you can add the remaining five OptionButtons without the need to reselect it on the Toolbox.
- Select the CommandButton on the Toolbox while the **Ctrl** button is pressed and add the two buttons.

The next stage is to change the caption of the form, the OptionButtons and the CommandButtons:

- Select the form by clicking anywhere on the form which is not occupied by a control.

- Change the **Caption** property to *Displaying Pictures.*
- Select the Frame and change its **Caption** property to *Choose a Sport.*
- Select the OptionButtons in turn and change their **Caption** properties to those shown in figure 4.1.
- Select the CommandButtons in turn and change their **Caption** properties.

To improve the appearance of the application, the fonts used have been changed:

- Press the **Ctrl** button and select all of the OptionButtons except for the *Browse* button.
- Click on the **Font** property in the Properties window and change the font to **MS Sans Serif**; change the size to 12 point in the Font dialog.
- Select the *Browse* button alone and change its **Font** property to **MS Sans Serif**, 12 point, **Bold Italic**.
- Select the Frame and change its **Font** property to **MS Sans Serif**, 12 point.

This is the point at which it is best to resize and move the controls to their correct positions. Your complete form should look like the one shown in figure 4.1.

Adding a new form

Most Visual Basic applications have one form, the majority have many forms. To add a form to your applications:

- Select the **Project | Add Form** menu item to display the Add Form dialog.

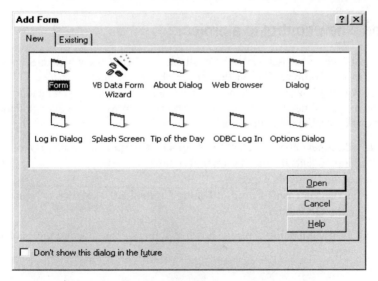

Figure 4.2 Adding a new form to an application.

- Choose the **New** page as shown in figure 4.2.
- Select the **Form** option.

- Click on the **Open** button.

A new form with a default name of *Form2* is added to your project.

You can switch between the two forms using the Project Explorer, or by clicking on the form which you want to use, if you can see a portion of it.

We do not want *Form2* to have a title bar, borders or scroll bars, since we do not want to be able to close it while the application is running. To achieve this select the new form and set its **BorderStyle** property to **None**.

This is a good time to specify the positions in which the two forms will appear when the application is run by using the Form Layout dialog as shown in figure 4.3.

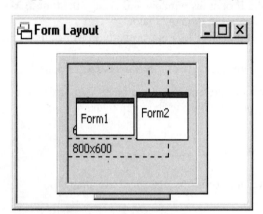

Figure 4.3 *The Form Layout dialog.*

Adding a new control to a project

The controls we have used so far are all intrinsic controls which are automatically available in the Toolbox. When the *Browse* button is clicked an open file dialog is displayed which allows you to view the files available on your system and to select one. To achieve this we need to add a custom control icon to the Toolbox and then add a copy of that control to the application:

- To add a new control select the **Project | Components** menu option to display the Components dialog as shown in figure 4.4.
- Select the **Controls** page.
- Select the **Microsoft CommonDialog Control 6.0**, as shown in figure 4.4.
- Click the **OK** button.

The new CommonDialog control, shown in figure 4.5, is added to the Toolbox.

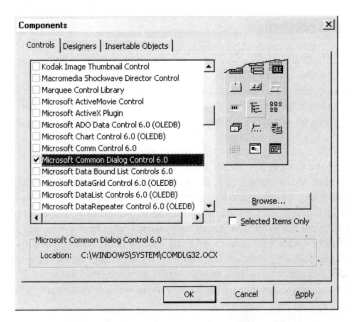

Figure 4.4 *Adding a new control to the Toolbox.*

Add a CommonDialog control to *Form1* of the application. It does not matter where you put it, since it is invisible at run–time. Even though it cannot be seen, it has a set of properties and methods which can be used.

 Figure 4.5 *The CommonDialog control.*

The completed form should look like the one shown in figure 4.6:

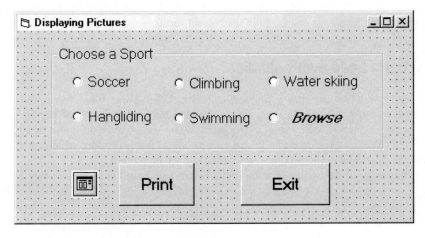

Figure 4.6 *The completed form at design–time.*

Naming the controls

All the controls in an application have names, that is have a **Name** property. If you wish you can rely on the default names which Visual Basic applies, for example *Command1* for the first CommandButton, *Command2* for the second and so on. However, it is better practice to give controls meaningful names, that will make sense to you if you return to the application later. In this application the CommandButtons and OptionButtons have been renamed.

The OptionButtons and CommandButtons have been given the same name as the text they display, for example *Soccer* for the first OptionButton and so on.

If you do change the names of controls in an application it is essential that you do so before creating any event procedures, since the name which Visual Basic gives to an event procedure is partially based on the name of the control, for example the handler for the click event for a button called *Command1* will be *Command1_Click*. If you change the name from *Command1* to *Exit*, Visual Basic will expect to find an event procedure called *Exit_Click*. The names of existing event procedures are not automatically changed to reflect changes in the names of controls. If you want to change the names of your controls it is best to do so first before any event procedures are written.

Handling events

If you run the application, only the main form appears and the buttons do not do anything. To make them functional we need to write some Visual Basic instructions. In a Windows environment whenever you take some action such as clicking on a button, or selecting an OptionButton, an event occurs. The Visual Basic application detects that event and executes an event procedure, which is a collection of Visual Basic instructions. You can add your own Visual Basic code to the event procedure to take some action, for example when the *Swimming* OptionButton is clicked the corresponding picture is displayed in the second form.

The Form Load event handler

The first event we are going to look at is the Load event for a form. When the application starts to run, the main form is loaded into memory and displayed. When this occurs a Form Load event is triggered. The event procedure for this event is executed. We need to add some Visual Basic code to this procedure which instructs the application to display the second form which shows the pictures.

At this stage in the application the Project Explorer should be similar to figure 4.7.

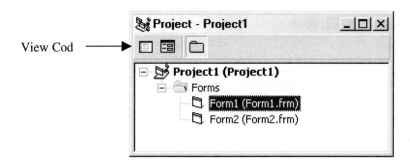

View Cod

Figure 4.7 The Project Explorer.

For every form there is a corresponding set of event procedures, which are contained in a single module. Every form has its own module which contains its own event procedures. To write the event procedure click on the **View Code** icon on the Project Explorer. You can return to the design form by clicking on the **View Object** icon which is adjacent to it. The focus of the application is now on the code window.

There are two drop down lists at the top of the code window:

- The left list gives all of the components available on this form. Since there is only one form per code module, whatever you call your form it will still appear as Form in this list.
- The right list gives all the events which the selected component can produce. In this case we want to work with the Load event.

Visual Basic now creates the outline event procedure for this event procedure:

Private Sub Form_Load( )

......

End Sub

- The reserved word **Private** means that this event procedure is only available to other procedures within the same module.
- The word **Sub** means that this is the start of a procedure (this is an historical hangover and stands for subroutine). A procedure is a collection of statements which has a name and allows them to be treated as a block.
- The name of the event procedure comes next. This is always made up of the name of the component, an underscore and the name of the event. The open and close brackets are mandatory. In some procedures information can be passed to the procedure within the brackets.
- The words **End Sub** mark the end of the event procedure.

We need to add a line of code to this event procedure to display the second form:

Form2.Show

At this stage the code window should be similar to figure 4.8.

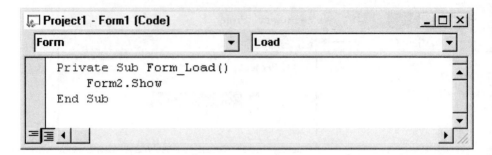

Figure 4.8 *The Form Load event procedure.*

One of the best features of Visual Basic is that you can test your application at any time simply by clicking on the run icon. If you run this application (you do not need to return to the design form) both of the forms will appear in the position specified by the Form Layout window. The buttons will not work yet since we have not added any code to the event procedures for the OptionButtons and CommandButtons.

The Quick Info facility

One very useful feature when you start to enter your code is that Visual Basic provides hints or tips which help you to write syntactically correct code. There are three types of assistance provided:

- Parameters for methods and functions.
- Properties and methods of an object.
- A list of acceptable constants.

In figure 4.9, this Quick Info feature indicates that the **Val** function requires a single string as its input parameter and returns a double value.

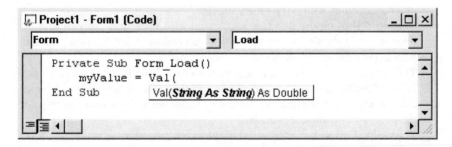

Figure 4.9 *Method and function parameters.*

When you type the name of any object the properties of that object are listed, as shown in figure 4.10.

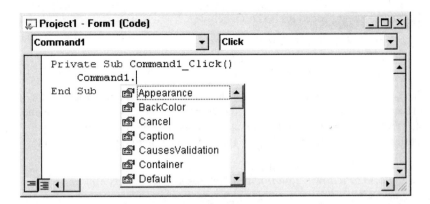

Figure 4.10 *Object properties.*

When you are intending to assign the property of a object, a list of possible values is displayed as shown in figure 4.11. If you wish to insert one of the possible options into your code, click on that option, or move to it by using the arrowed keys and press the **Tab** key.

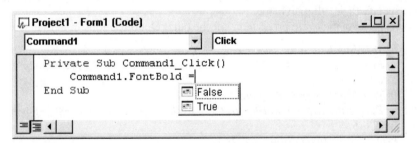

Figure 4.11 *List of acceptable constants.*

You can turn these feature off using the **Editor** page of the **Tools I Options** menu. Click on three check boxes: **Auto List Members**, **Auto Quick Info** and **Auto Data Tips**, so that they are not checked. It is recommended that you leave these very useful facilities working.

If you do turn these features off, you can still use them occasionally by right clicking in the code window to display the speed menu and choosing the appropriate options.

The OptionButton event handlers

We need to add event handlers for the OptionButtons, so that when a button is selected the corresponding picture is displayed.

To create the template event procedure:

- Select *Soccer* from the list of controls in the left menu on the code window.
- Select **Click** from the list of events in the right menu.

The outline event procedure is shown below:

> ***Private Sub** Soccer_Click( )*
> *......*
> ***End Sub***

This is exactly the same format as for the Form Load event: as expected, the name of the procedure comprises the name of the control, an underscore and the name of the event. To load the corresponding image we must change the **Picture** property of the second form. We can do this using the **LoadPicture** function as shown below:

> ***Private Sub** Soccer_Click( )*
> *   **Form2.Picture** = **LoadPicture**("c:\DisplayingPictures\Soccer.bmp")*
> ***End Sub***

When you want to change the property of a control or a form you must specify its name, in this case *Form2*, followed by a period and the name of the property, **Picture**.

The **LoadPicture** function takes the name of a picture file as a parameter, note that the name must be enclosed in double quotes. Overall the **LoadPicture** function reads a picture from the file and assigns it to the **Picture** property of *Form2*.

If you want to try this application for yourself you will need to use your own pictures and to specify their full path name.

You can create the event procedures for the other OptionButtons in the same way:

> ***Private Sub** Climbing_Click( )*
> *   **Form2.Picture** = **LoadPicture**("c:\DisplayingPictures\Climbing.bmp")*
> ***End Sub***
> ***Private Sub** WaterSkiing_Click( )*
> *   **Form2.Picture** = **LoadPicture**("c:\DisplayingPictures\WaterSkiing.bmp")*
> ***End Sub***
> ***Private Sub** HangGliding_Click( )*
> *   **Form2.Picture** = **LoadPicture**("c:\DisplayingPictures\Hangliding.bmp")*
> ***End Sub***
> ***Private Sub** Swimming_Click( )*
> *   **Form2.Picture** = **LoadPicture**("c:\DisplayingPictures\Swimming.bmp")*
> ***End Sub***

There is one OptionButton we have not dealt with which has the caption *Browse*. This opens a file dialog and allows you to browse through your system and to select a file. The event procedure for this control is:

> ***Private Sub** Browse_Click( )*
> *   CommonDialog1.**ShowOpen***
> *   **Form2.Picture** = **LoadPicture**(CommonDialog1.**FileName**)*
> ***End Sub***

The **ShowOpen** method of *CommonDialog1* displays the Open File dialog as shown in figure 4.12.

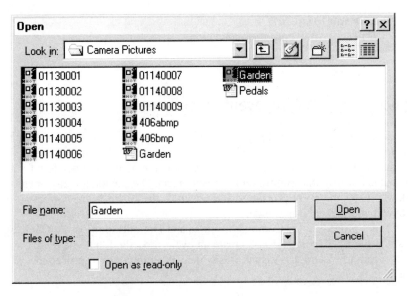

Figure 4.12 The Open File dialog.

You can browse through your file system and select a file. When you click on the **Open** button, the name of the file selected is saved in the **FileName** property of the CommonDialog. This file name is assigned to the **Picture** property of *Form2* and the image selected is displayed.

If you run the application now, the OptionButtons are functioning and you can display any of the five pre–selected files or browse to find another file to display.

The CommandButton event handlers

The final stage is to add the event handlers for the *Print* and *Exit* buttons. Create the event handler for the click events of these two buttons in the usual way. Visual Basic has a simple way of printing the entire content of a form, using the **PrintForm** method. To use it, specify the name of the form to be printed, a period character and then the method name, **PrintForm**. The whole event procedure for the *Print* button is shown below

> *Private Sub Print_Click( )*
>   *Form2.PrintForm*
> *End Sub*

The printer used is the default printer specified by the Control Panel settings.

The results of printing may be disappointing, since the **PrintForm** method takes a pixel–by–pixel copy of the form. The resolution of the whole screen is probably 1024×768, much less than the resolution of a typical printer which is 600×600 per inch.

When the *Exit* button is clicked its click event procedure is run. The **End** statement closes the two forms and ends the application. The event procedure is shown below:

> ***Private Sub** Exit_Click( )*
>   ***End***   ' ends the application
> ***End Sub***

A quick way of making event procedures

There is a short cut to making the most common event procedures, rather than displaying the code window and selecting the control and the type of event procedure you want. All you have to do to create the most common event procedure for a control is to double click on that control on the design form. This automatically opens the code window, creates the event procedure and positions the cursor in the correct position for you to add your Visual Basic code.

The event procedure for CommandButtons and OptionButtons is the Click event, for forms it is the Load event. If you create an event procedure that you do not want, you do not need to delete it: Visual Basic deletes empty event procedures when the application is run.

Saving your application

When your application is complete you can save it using the **File | Save Project As** menu option. This prompts for the name of each file in the project as shown in figure 4.13, and finally the name of the project file, which maintains a list of all of the components of the project.

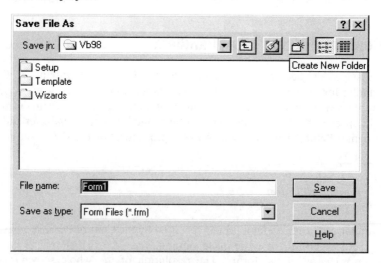

Figure 4.13 *Saving the project.*

It is a good idea to save every application you write in a separate folder, since it makes it easier to see which files are included within a project, and if you rely on the default file names the latest application you write does not overwrite previous applications. When you are saving your project you will be prompted for the name of each of the files in a project, in this case the two forms, as shown in figure 4.13. If you wish you can create a new folder, if you are unsure of which button to press to do this the tool–tip facility displays a message indicating the function of the buttons as you move the cursor over them. The form and the associated event procedures are both saved.

If you make changes to the application, you can save those changes by using the **File | Save Project** menu option.

Making an executable file

The application we have created has only been run within the Visual Basic environment. If you want to run this application on its own, without Visual Basic, you need to create a Windows executable file that is a file with an EXE extension. To do this select the **File | Make Project1.exe** menu option. You can then run this file directly, or make a copy and run it on another computer, which may not have the Visual Basic IDE.

5
Controlling Program Flow

Introduction

One of the key features of Visual Basic, in common with other programming languages is the ability to make decisions on the basis of information. For example, if you are writing an application for calculating the cost of car insurance and a person gives his age as 18, the premiums will be higher than for an older person: the application calculates a different cost depending on age. In the last chapter we saw how to respond to the events which occur when an application runs, but we did not see how to take these sorts of decisions, that is how to control the program flow.

There are three language constructs for controlling program flow:

- **If..Then..Else**
- **Select Case**
- **GoTo**

In this chapter we are going to look at these constructs and also some new controls, methods and functions.

Adding comments

When you try this application is helpful to add comments to your Visual Basic code, to help you remember what a event procedure does, or to explain a complex piece of code. To add a comment, use the ' character. The remainder of the line will be ignored by Visual Basic and you can type whatever text you wish.

```
' This is a line of comment
Form1.Show                    ' and this text is also comment
```

If you want to have more than one line of comments you must add the comment symbol at the start of every line.

There are no firm rules about where you should add comments, most companies have their own guidelines, but generally it is helpful to add comments at the start of an event procedure and wherever the code is not clear:

> **Unload** *Form2*   ' *unload form2*

The comment in the line above is not very helpful, but another programmer looking at the line of code below would be pleased to have the comment:

> *Form1.***BackColor** = *&HFF0000*   ' *make background blue*

Spreading a statement over multiple lines

Sometimes a statement is too long to fit conveniently on to one line. You can spread it over more than one line by adding the line continuation character _ at the end of the line.

> *Form2.***Picture** = _
> **LoadPicture**(*"c:\DisplayingPictures\Climbing.bmp"*)

You cannot use the continuation character on a line where the comment character is used.

More than one statement to a line

You can put more than one statement on the same line using the : character:

> **Unload** *Form1:* **Unload** *Form2:* **Unload** *Form3*

This can make the code less readable and so it is not a good idea to use this facility.

The ComboBox and Image controls

The application we are going to develop next is shown in figure 5.1 and uses the ComboBox and Image controls. You can select one of the sports shown in the combo box; the corresponding picture is displayed in an Image control and a Label control displays the name of the sport selected.

Before developing this application we need to look at the combo box which allows you to choose the sport.

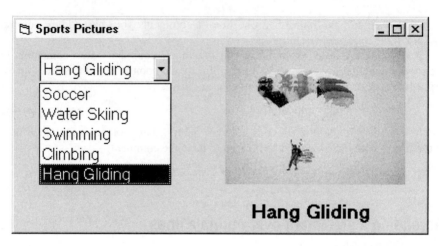

Figure 5.1 *The running application.*

The ComboBox control

The ComboBox control, shown in figure 5.2, has three distinct types controlled by the **Style** property.

    Figure 5.2 *The ComboBox control.*

The **Style** property can have three possible values:

- Dropdown combo ~ the **Style** property has a value of **vbComboDropDown** which is a constant and has a value of 0. This version has a text box and a list which drops down below it. You can select an item from the list or type your own text in the text box.
- Simple combo ~ the **Style** property is **vbComboSimple** which is 1. This version comprises a text box and a list which does not drop down. You can select an item or type your own text. The default size shows only one item, but you can change it at design–time or run–time.
- Dropdown List combo ~ the **Style** property is **vbComboDrop–DropList**, which is 2. This is the same as a dropdown combo except that while you can select an item from the list you cannot type your own text.

The three different styles are shown in figure 5.3.

Figure 5.3 Dropdown, simple and dropdown list combos.

The form which we want to use in this application is the Dropdown List combo, since this allows you to select an item, but not to type your own text.

Creating an application

The first stage is to add the Image, ComboBox and Label controls to the design form, so they are roughly in the positions shown in figure 5.1.

The next stage is to set up some properties at design–time.

- The **Name** property of the Image control is changed to *Pic*. The ComboBox is changed to *Sport* and the Label is changed to *SportName*.
- The **Font** property of the ComboBox is changed to 12 point Sans Serif plain.
- The **Font** of the Label is changed to 14 point Sans Serif bold.
- The **Alignment** property of the Label is changed to **Center**, so that the text is in the middle of its display area.
- The ComboBox **Style** property is changed to a Dropdown List combo.
- The **Caption** property of the form is changed to *Sport Pictures*.
- The **Stretch** property of the Image control is changed to **True**, so that the picture resizes itself to fit the control.

You can add the options which are displayed in the ComboBox at design–time by using the **List** property, but we are going to do this at run–time using some Visual Basic statements.

Using the ComboBox control

The best place to add items to the ComboBox control is when the Form Load event occurs. The **AddItem** method of the ComboBox does this. The format used when applying methods is always the same: the name of the control, followed by a period and the name of the method. If any parameters are needed by the method they are specified next; if more than one parameter is specified they are separated by commas. To add the text *Soccer* to the ComboBox called *Sport:*

   *Sport.**AddItem** "Soccer"*

Additional uses of the **AddItem** method add further entries to the ComboBox.

There is an optional second parameter which can follow the first which specifies the position in the ComboBox where the item is to be added, for example:

*Sport.**AddItem** "Swimming", 2*

Since the first item in the ComboBox is 0, the line above puts the text *Swimming* as the third entry.

When you click on an item in a ComboBox, the **ListIndex** property is set; by checking this property the application can find out what entry has been chosen. The text of the entry which has been selected is saved in the **List** property:

*Sport.**List**(0)*

contains the text representing the first item in the ComboBox list, in this case *Soccer*.

The complete code for the Form Load event which occurs when the application starts is shown below:

```
Private Sub Form_Load( )
    Sport.AddItem "Soccer"
    Sport.AddItem "Water skiing"
    Sport.AddItem "Swimming"
    Sport.AddItem "Climbing"
    Sport.AddItem "Hang gliding"
    Sport.ListIndex = 0
    SportName.Caption = Sport.List(Sport.ListIndex)
    Pic.Picture = LoadPicture("C:\UsingIfThenElse\Soccer.bmp")
End Sub
```

Five items are added to the ComboBox. The **ListIndex** property is assigned to zero, which selects the first item in the list. The **Caption** property of the Label is assigned the text represented by *Sport.**List**(0)*, which represents the first item in the list *Soccer*.

The **Picture** property of the **Image** control called **SportPicture** is assigned to the image stored in the specified file using the **LoadPicture** function. If you try this application you will need to specify the location and name of your own image files in the **LoadPicture** function.

It is a good idea to run the application at this stage, to see if the Visual Basic code you have added is correct. The *Soccer* picture should be displayed with the correct caption. All of the items will be available in the ComboBox, but selecting one of them does not make either the picture or its caption change.

The With statement

The *Form_Load* procedure shown above works correctly without problems, but it could be made easier to read by using a **With** statement, which allows you to perform a series of operations on an object without the need to refer repeatedly to that object ~ in the case of this procedure the *Sport* control. The general form is:

> **With** *object*
>   *statements*
> **End With**

The new event procedure becomes:

> **Private Sub** *Form_Load( )*
> **With** *Sport*
>   **.AddItem** *"Soccer"*
>   **.AddItem** *"Water skiing"*
>   **.AddItem** *"Swimming"*
>   **.AddItem** *"Climbing"*
>   **.AddItem** *"Hang gliding"*
>   **.ListIndex** = *0*
> **End With**
>   *SportName.***Caption** = *Sport.***List***(Sport.***ListIndex***)*
>   *Pic.***Picture** = **LoadPicture***("C:\UsingIfThenElse\Soccer.bmp")*
> **End Sub**

Functionally this is the same as before but is easier to read and there is less typing.

Using the If..Then..Else statement

When an item is selected from the ComboBox called *Sport*, a click event occurs. We need to test the **ListIndex** property of this control and display a different picture and text depending on its value. To do this we can use the **If..Then** statement. The basic form of this statement is:

> **If** *condition* **Then** *statement*

for example:

> **If** *Sport.***ListIndex** = *0* **Then** *Pic.***Picture** = **LoadPicture***("Soccer.bmp")*

This tests the value of the **ListIndex** property. If it is zero, the first item in the list has been selected, and the statement assigning the **Picture** property of the Image control called *Pic* to the soccer picture is executed. If the **ListIndex** value is not zero the statement following the **Then** clause is not executed.

This form of the **If..Then** statement is fine if you only want to execute one statement if the condition is met. If you want to execute a number of statements you can use a slightly different syntax:

> **If** *condition* **Then**
>   *statements*   ' *as many statements as you wish can go here*
> **End If**

If..Then..Else statements tend to be long and you can use this syntax to spread the statement over several lines:

```
If Sport.ListIndex = 0 Then
    Pic.Picture = LoadPicture("Soccer.bmp")
End If
```

This is functionally exactly the same as the single line version.

If you want to test a number of values you can extend the **If..Then** statement by adding an **Else** clause. The basic form of this statement is:

```
If condition Then statement Else
If condition Then statement Else
... ... ...
```

You can add as many **If..Then..Else** clauses as you wish, however many you add a maximum of one of them is executed. If none of the **If** conditions are met, none of the statements are executed, for example:

```
If Sport.ListIndex = 0 Then Pic.Picture = LoadPicture("Soccer.bmp") Else
If Sport.ListIndex = 1 Then Pic.Picture = LoadPicture("WaterSkiing.bmp")
```

Since the path name of the folder where the picture files are stored is long, the **ChDir** statement is used to change the current path name to the folder where the files are stored. The complete code for the click event for the *Sport* ComboBox is shown below:

```
Private Sub Sport_Click( )
ChDir "C:\UsingIfThenElse"
 If Sport.ListIndex = 0 Then Pic.Picture = LoadPicture("Soccer.bmp") Else
If Sport.ListIndex = 1 Then Pic.Picture = LoadPicture("WaterSkiing.bmp") _
Else
If Sport.ListIndex = 2 Then Pic.Picture = LoadPicture("Swimming.bmp") Else
If Sport.ListIndex = 3 Then Pic.Picture = LoadPicture("Climbing.bmp") Else
If Sport.ListIndex = 4 Then Pic.Picture = LoadPicture("HangGliding.bmp")
SportName.Caption = Sport.List(Sport.ListIndex)
End Sub
```

Note the continuation character at the end of the fourth line which allows the **Else** keyword to be put on to the following line. The **Caption** property of the label *SportName* is assigned the text of the currently selected item in the ComboBox.

Using the Select Case statement

The **Select Case** statement is a useful alternative to using **If..Then..Else** statements, it is often easier to read. The basic form of this statement is:

```
Select Case test expression
    Case expression list1
        statement block1
    Case expression list 2
        statement block2
    ......
    Case Else
```

Statement block n
End Select

The event procedure below is functionally identical to the *Sport_Click* event procedure in the previous application, but is easier to read.

```
Private Sub Sport_Click( )
    ChDir "C:\books\vb\v6.0\UsingIfThenElse"
    SportName.Caption = Sport.List(Sport.ListIndex)
    Select Case Sport.ListIndex
        Case 0
            Pic.Picture = LoadPicture("Soccer.bmp")
        Case 1
            Pic.Picture = LoadPicture("WaterSkiing.bmp")
        Case 2
            Pic.Picture = LoadPicture("Swimming.bmp")
        Case 3
            Pic.Picture = LoadPicture("Climbing.bmp")
        Case 4
            Pic.Picture = LoadPicture("HangGliding.bmp")
    End Select
End Sub
```

There are a number of restrictions on how **Select..Case** statements can be used the test expression must be one of the following:

- A string or numeric expression.
- An explicit value.
- A range using the keyword **To.**
- A conditional range using the keyword **Is.**

The application shown below in figure 5.4 uses a **Select..Case** statement with the **To** and **Is** qualifiers. You type the amount of memory on your computer and a message box is displayed stating whether you have enough memory or not.

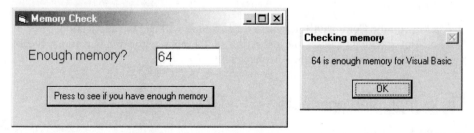

Figure 5.4 *Have you got enough memory?*

The code for this application is shown below:

```
Private Sub Command1_Click( )
    If IsNumeric(Text1.Text) Then    ' if a number input check the memory
```

```
        Select Case CInt(Text1.Text)
        Case Is < 16
            MsgBox (Text1.Text + " is far too little memory for Visual Basic")
        Case 16 To 32
            MsgBox (Text1.Text + " is too little memory for Visual Basic")
        Case 48, 64
            MsgBox (Text1.Text + " is enough memory for Visual Basic")
        Case Is > 64
            MsgBox (Text1.Text + " is ample memory for Visual Basic")
        End Select
    Else
        MsgBox ("Input a number")        ' A non integer has been typed
    End If
End Sub
```

There are a few new elements which we have not seen before. The **IsNumeric** function returns **True** if the text typed into *Text1* can be converted to an integer. If it can the **Select**..**Case** statement is executed. The text typed is actually converted into an integer using the **CInt** function. Depending on the amount of memory you have specified, a message box, with an **OK** button, is displayed using the **MsgBox** function. The text displayed in the message box is specified in the brackets following the function name. The title on the message box is the project title, although we shall see later how to specify the title and the buttons which are displayed.

Closing an application

You can close the application by clicking on the close icon in the top right corner of the window. If, perhaps, you want to close the application by clicking on a button, you can use the **End** statement, for example:

```
    Private Sub ExitButton_Click( )
        End
    End Sub
```

Clicking on the CommandButton called *ExitButton* will end the application.

The **Stop** statement pauses the execution of the application and puts it into break mode for debugging as we will see in chapter 13.

The comparison operators

In addition to checking two values for equality, which we have seen in previous examples, Visual Basic provides a comprehensive set of operators for testing other relationships between values as shown in table 5.1.

Table 5.1 *The comparison operators.*

Operator	Action
=	Equal.
<	Less than.
>	Greater than.
<=	Less than or equal.
>=	Greater than or equal.
<>	Not equal.

These operators can be used on strings as well as numeric values.

Looping

Some of the most common programming structures in Visual Basic are the looping constructs: these allow you to repeat a block of code many times, perhaps changing the value of a variable each time. There are three types of construct:

- **While..Wend**
- **Do..Loop**
- **For..Next**

The While..Wend statement

This statement tests a condition and if it is met , executes a series of statements. The general form is:

> **While** *condition*
> *statements*   *' as many statements as you wish*
> **Wend**

The next application we are going to look at uses this construct to find out if a number is prime, that is if a number which is input can be divided by any number apart from 1 and itself and leave no remainder.

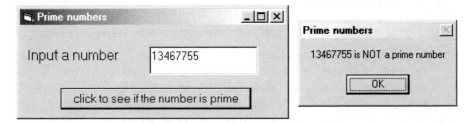

Figure 5.5 *Checking to see if a number is prime.*

The running application is shown in figure 5.5. The result is displayed in a message box. The complete code for this application is shown below:

```
Private Sub Command1_Click( )
' a prime number can only be divided by itself and 1 and leave no remainder
    If IsNumeric(Text1.Text) Then
        ' number is a long representation of text1.text
        number = CLng(Text1.Text)
        d = number - 1
        prime = True
        While (d > 1)
            ' if there is no remainder after division, the variable number can be
            ' divided exactly by d, and is therefore not a prime
            If number Mod d = 0 Then prime = False
            d = d - 1
        Wend
        If prime Then MsgBox (Text1.Text + " is a prime number") Else
        If Not prime Then MsgBox (Text1.Text + " is NOT a prime number")
    End If
End Sub
```

A check is made to see if the text typed into the text field is a valid number using the **IsNumeric** function. If it is a number, it is assigned to the variable *number* as a **Long** integer value using the **CLng** function. This function is used rather than the **CInt** function which converts to an integer since **Long** variables can represent larger values than the **Integer** type.

The technique used to see if *number* is prime is not very sophisticated or efficient. It simply divides *number* by every integer between *number* - 1 and 2. The **Mod** operator is used to do this, because it returns the remainder after division. If this is zero, the boolean *prime* is set to **False** since if a number can be divided exactly by another number it is not prime. Every time the **While..Wend** loop is executed, the value of the variable *d* is decreases by 1 until the test condition is no longer met and *d* is not greater than 1. A message box is then displayed depending on the state of the *prime* boolean variable.

The Do..While statement

The **Do..While** statement is functionally the same as the **While..Wend** statement.
The general form is:

```
Do While condition
    statements              ' as many statements as you wish
Loop
```

The code below could be used to replace the **While..Wend** loop in the previous example.

> **Do While** *(d > 1)*
>   **If** *number* **Mod** *d = 0* **Then** *prime* = **False**
>   *d = d - 1*
> **Loop**

Functionally the application is the same as before.

You can reverse the form of this statement and place the test condition at the end:

> **Do**
>   *statements*   *' as many statements as you wish*
> **Loop While** *condition*

You can exit from a **Do** loop before it has completed by issuing the **Exit..Do** statement.

The Do..Until statement

This is a variation of the **Do..Loop** statement. Its general form is:

> **Do Until** *condition*
>   *statements*   *' as many statements as you wish*
>   **Exit Do**   *' this optional statement exits the loop*
>   *statements*   *' as many statements as you wish*
> **Loop**

The body of this loop is executed until the specified condition is met. The code below is functionally the same as the loop in the previous examples and could be used in its place. Note the changed test condition at the start of the loop.

> **Do Until** *(d <= 1)*
>   **If** *number* **Mod** *d = 0* **Then** *prime* = **False**
>   *d = d - 1*
> **Loop**

A variation on this statement is to put the condition at the end:

> **Do**
>   *statements*   *' as many statements as you wish*
> **Loop Until** *condition*

You can exit from this loop before it has completed with an **Exit..Do** statement

The For..Next statement

It is quite common to increase or decrease a counter within a loop and Visual Basic provides a statement which does this. The general form of the **For..Next** loop is:

> **For** *counter = start* **To** *end* **Step** *value*
>   *statements*   *' as many statements as you wish*
>   **Exit For**   *' this optional statement exits from the loop*

> *statements*   ' *as many statements as you wish*
> **Next**   ' *increase the counter and go to start of loop*

The counter is a numerical value which is assigned the start value the first time the loop is executed. The loop continues until the counter has reached the end value. If you wish you can specify the reserved word **Step** and a value. Every time the loop is executed the counter has this value added to it. The step value can be positive or negative. If you omit the **Step** reserved word and its value, the counter is increased by one every time the loop is exited.

The following statements can replace the loops in the previous examples; note that there is no need to give the variable *d* a value before the loop, since it is initialised by the **For** statement itself.

> **For** *d = number - 1* **To** *2* **Step** *-1*
> **If** *number* **Mod** *d = 0* **Then** *prime =* **False**
> **Next** *d*

This **For..Next** statement is more compact than the other loops and wherever you wish to have a counter this type of loop is the best one to use.

6

Variables and Operators

Introduction

In most programming languages when we want to represent a piece of data within an application we need to decide what type it is. For example, the number of people working in a company is likely to be a whole number, that is an integer; the balance of a bank account is represent by a variable of a currency type, and so on. Visual Basic is one of the few languages which allow you to use variables without first declaring what type they are. Visual Basic does offer you the option of declaring the type of variables before using them, and there are some important benefits to doing this. The type of a variable determines what operations you can carry out on it, for example you cannot multiply a text string.

Visual Basic has a very rich set of data types and variables which we are going to look at in this chapter.

Naming conventions

Variable names must conform to these rules:

- Must begin with a letter.
- Must not contain an embedded period of one of the type declaration characters (for example $).
- Must be 255 characters or less.
- Must be unique within its scope.

The use of the type declaration characters and the scope of a variable is described later in this chapter.

Variable types

Visual Basic offers an extensive range of twelve data types as shown in table 6.1.

Table 6.1 Data types.

Type	Size in bytes	Suffix
Boolean	2	No suffix.
Byte	1	No suffix.
Currency	8	@
Date	8	No suffix.
Decimal	14	No suffix.
Integer	2	%
Long	4	&
Object	4	No suffix.
Single	4	!
Double	8	#
String	Dependent on string size.	$
Variant	Dependent on type of data stored.	None.

If these data types are not sufficient you can define your own.

There are two ways of defining the type of a variable explicitly: you can either use **Dim** or its variants or for some types you can follow the name by a suffix, for example *Value%* is an **Integer**, while *MyLine$* is a **String**.

Declaring variables

One of the most common mistakes in Visual Basic is to misspell the name of a variable. This does not cause a syntax error, but the program does not behave as expected. One way around this is to declare the name and type of variables prior to their first use; the **Dim** statement is used for this, for example:

> *Dim Value **As Integer**, Total **As Single***

The general form is:

> *Dim identifier **As** type, identifier **As** type......*

It is a good idea to make variable declaration mandatory by either:

- Selecting the **Tools | Options** menu option, displaying the **Editor** page and checking the **Require Variable Declaration** CheckBox as shown in figure 6.1.
- If you only want to force explicit declarations in one module, put the following line into the General section of the module:

> *Option Explicit*

To go to the General section of a module display the code window and select the **(General)** option from the dropdown list of objects on the top left of the window.

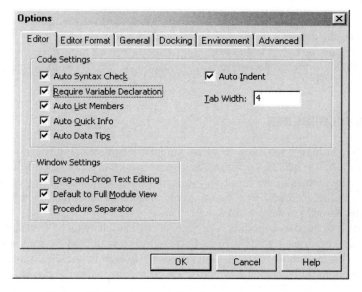

Figure 6.1 *Making variable declaration mandatory.*

Static variables

There are a number of other issues to be considered when you are declaring a variable. A variable declared within a procedure is initialised every time the procedure is entered. However, if you want a variable to retain its value and not be re–initialised the **Static** keyword must be used in place of **Dim**:

> ***Static*** *identifier* ***As*** *type*

For example:

> ***Static*** *Counter* ***As Integer***

Variable scope

The scope of a variable, that is how visible it is to procedures in the application, depends on where it is declared:

- A variable declared in a procedure with **Dim** or **Static** is only available for use within that procedure..
- A variable declared in the General section of the a module with the keyword **Private** is available to all procedures in that module.

- A variable declared in the General section of a module with the keyword **Public** is available to all procedures in all modules.

for example:

> *' General section*
> **Private** *intValue* **As Integer**   *' available to all procedures in the module*
> **Public** *intResult* **As Integer**   *' available throughout the application*

Declaring constants

Sometimes you may want to use a value which will not change throughout the life of the application. Visual Basic makes extensive use of constants in its functions, for defining many aspects of the function, for example the buttons displayed on a dialog to a standard set of colours. To define your own constant values, which cannot be changed, the **Const** keyword is used.

A constant defined in a module is private to that module, while a constant defined in the General section may be defined as **Private** in the same way as a variable. If you wish to define a **Public** constant you can only do this in the General section of a standard module, not a module which is connected to a form and handles its event procedures. You can add a standard module to your project by choosing the **Project |
Add Module** menu option and selecting the **Module** icon.

> *' General section*
> **Private Const** *intValue* **As Integer** = *42*
> **Private Const** *pi* **As Double** = *3.142*

To create a **Public** constant:

> *' General section of a standard module*
> **Public Const** *distance* **As Double** = *382.97*

You can also combine declarations on to one line:

> *' Declaration in a module, implicitly private*
> **Const** *myInt* **As Integer** = *7, MyString* = *"System failure imminent"*

You do not have to explicitly state the type of the constant, for example in the declaration of *MyString* above, but it is better to do so.

The Boolean data type

The **Boolean** type is used for data which can have only one of two possible values, for example **True / False** or **Yes / No** type variables. Booleans can be assigned using the keywords **True** and **False**.

If you convert a numeric type such as an **Integer**, a value of 0 becomes a **False Boolean**, all other values are **True**.

If you convert from a **Boolean** to a numeric type, **False** becomes 0 and **True** -1.

Data types representing integers

There are three data types which are used for representing integers: **Byte**, **Integer** and **Long**. The type you choose to use is dependent on the range of numbers you want to use. The greater the range of numbers which can be stored, the greater the space required by the variable.

You can make a variable an **Integer** by placing the % character at the end of its name. You can declare a **Long** using the & character in the same way, for example:

```
PointsScored% = 15            ' an Integer
MilesToMars& = 20000000       ' a Long
```

Data types representing floating point numbers

There are four data types which can represent floating point numbers: **Single, Double, Currency** and **Decimal**.

The single floating point type which should be used where accuracy is not paramount. Operations are still relatively quick on this type, although much slower than on the integer types. The suffix indicating a **Single** value is !, for a **Double** the character is #, for example:

```
AverageTemperatureOfHawaii! = 25.3    ' degrees centigrade as a Single
pi# = 3.141592                        ' Double value
```

As the name suggests the **Currency** type should be used for calculations involving money, or where accuracy is particularly important. Values are stored in this type as an integer scaled by 10,000 to give a fixed point type with fifteen digits on the left of the decimal point and four on the right. The suffix for the **Currency** type is @, for example:

```
LoadsOfMoney@ = 675876.87
```

The **Decimal** data type is the largest and most accurate of the floating point types. It stores values an integer scaled by a power of ten between 10^0 and 10^{28}.

You cannot declare a variable to belong to the **Decimal** type directly; however, you can coerce a **Variant** data type to be a **Decimal** using the **CDec** function, for example:

```
Value! = 23.2          ' a Single value
Cost = CDec(Value)     ' Cost is Decimal
```

The **Variant** data type is covered later in this chapter.

The Date data type

The **Date** type does not have a suffix, but when assigning a date to a variable of this type, the date is enclosed between two # characters, for example:

```
ChristmasEve = #24/12/99#
```

You can add integers to a date, for example:

ChristmasDay = ChristmasEve + 1

Two useful function are **Now** which returns the current date and time and **Date** which returns the current date, for example:

*TodaysDateandTime = **Now***
*TodaysDate = **Date***

The Object data type

The **Object** type is used to address an object. You can use the **Set** statement to connect two objects as shown below:

```
Private Sub Command1_Click( )
    Set MyObject = Text1
    ' MyObject and Text1 refer to the same object
    MyObject.Text = "MyObject and Text1 now refer to the same object"
    Text2.Text = MyObject.Text
    Text2.BackColor = MyObject.BackColor
    ' break the reference to Text1
    Set MyObject = Nothing
End Sub
```

In the example application, shown running in figure 6.2, *MyObject* and *Text1* refer to the same object, therefore any changes made to *MyObject* are automatically made to *Text1*.

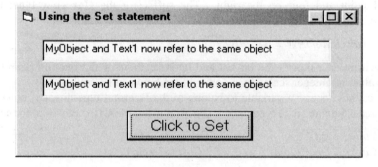

*Figure 6.2 Using the **Set** statement to associate objects.*

Changing the **Text** property of *MyObject* changes the **Text** property of *Text1*. Assigning the **Text** and **BackColor** properties of *MyObject* to *Text2* ensures that these two properties are the same for *Text1* and *Text2*. The association between *Text1* and *MyObject* is broken by assigning *MyObject* to the keyword **Nothing**.

The String data type

This data type is used to contain a sequence of characters. You can concatenate strings using the & operator, for example:

> *FirstName$ = "Thelma"*
> *SecondName$ = "Louise"*
> *Text2.Text = "It's " & FirstName$ & " and " & SecondName$*

You can also use the + operator to concatenate strings, but this can cause some problems where the strings to be concatenated could be converted to numeric values, for example:

> *Text1.Text = 7 + 8*   *' add*
> *Text2.Text = 7 & 8*   *' concatenate*

The TextBox *Text1* will display 15, the result of adding 7 and 8, while *Text2* will display 78, the result of concatenating the two strings.

You can use the type identifier character, $, to indicate that a variable is a **String**, or use a **Dim** or **Static** statement to declare it. The length of the **String** will change so that it is just big enough to store the text; however, if you wish you can specify that a **String** will always have a size by specifying this in the declaration statement, for example:

> **Dim** *Name* **As String** * *40*

The **String** *Name* will always be forty characters long.

The Variant data type

If you do not explicitly state the type of a data variable it is taken to be **Variant** data type. A **Variant** variable can contain any type of data (even data types you have defined yourself) except for a fixed length **String**. If you assign a variable of any type to a **Variant**, the **Variant** adopts that type. If, for example, you assign an **Integer** to a **Variant**, all subsequent operations treat the **Variant** as an **Integer**. If you carry out arithmetic which produces a result which cannot be stored in an **Integer**, the **Variant** takes on the data type of the next largest type, in this case **Long**.

This type takes on the form of the data which it is asked to store. For example, if a string is assigned to a **Variant** type, the **Variant** type takes on the **String** data type. If it is assigned a numeric value, it takes on that type and can be used in calculations.

A **Variant** can contain four special values:

- **Empty**. Indicates that that it has not been assigned an initial value. It is not the same as 0, or the **String** "". You can test to see if a variable is **Empty** using the **IsEmpty** function which returns **True** if it is **Empty**, for example:

  If IsEmpty(FinalResult) **Then** *Text = "Empty"* **Else** *Text = "not empty"*

- **Null**. This value is used in database applications to indicate missing data. You can assign **Null** to a **Variant**. You can test to see if a **Variant** is **Null** using the

isNull function. An application never assigns **Null** to a **Variant** unless you explicitly do so, for example:

*MyVariant = **Null***

- **Nothing**. If the **Variant** has been assigned to an **Object** using the **Set** statement it can be disassociated from that **Object** by assigning it to **Nothing**, for example:

  *Set FinalResult = **Nothing***

- **Error**. Indicates that an error has occurred. You can assign an error value to a variant using the **CVErr** function and test to see if an error has been assigned using the **IsError** function. In the application below, a function has been defined called *DaysToChristmas*. This function is passed a date and it checks to see if it is a valid date using the **IsDate** function, and that the date is before Christmas 1999. If it is not the **CVErr** function is used to return an error. If there is not an error the number of days to Christmas is calculated and returned. The function is called when a button is clicked. If an error is returned the message *invalid date* is displayed in the Immediate window. If the date 5/5/1999 is passed to the function, the message *234 days to Christmas* is displayed. The complete listing is shown below:

```
Private Sub Command1_Click( )
    message = DaysToChristmas(#5/5/1999#)          'month day year
' display an error message or the number of days to Christmas
    If IsError(message) Then Debug.Print "invalid" Else Debug.Print message
End Sub
Function DaysToChristmas(myDate) As Variant
' returns the number of days to Christmas or an error
    ChristmasDay = #12/25/1999#
' if the date is invalid or after Christmas return an error
    If Not IsDate(myDate) Or myDate > ChristmasDay Then
        DaysToChristmas = CVErr(1001)
    Else
        DaysToChristmas = ChristmasDay - myDate & " days to Christmas"
    End If
End Function
```

The **Print** method of the **Debug** object, referred to by **Debug.Print**, is very useful when you want to print out messages on to the Immediate window to monitor the progress of your application or to display error messages.

The range of data types

The different data types can represent different ranges of values with different accuracies, depending on the format and the number of bytes used. The range of these types is shown in table 6.2.

Table 6.2 *The range of data types.*

Type	Most Negative	Most Positive
Byte	0	255
Boolean	Not applicable.	Not applicable.
Integer	-32,768	32,767
Long	-2,147,483,648	2,147,483,647
Double	-1.797 693 134 862 32 E308	1.797 693 134 862 32 E308
Currency	-922,337,203,685,477 ·5808	922,337,203,685,477 ·5807
Decimal	79228162414264337593543950335	79228162414264337593543950335
Date	Earliest : January 1 100.	Latest : December 31 9999.
Object	Not applicable.	Not applicable.
Single	-3.402 823 E38	3.402 823 E38
Variant (numbers)	Same as double.	Same as double.
Variant (string)	Not applicable.	Not applicable.
String	Not applicable.	Approx. 65,400 characters.

Converting between data types

Sometimes you may need to convert from one data type to another, Visual Basic provides a comprehensive set of functions which allow you to do this as listed in table 6.3.

Table 6.3 *Functions for converting between data types.*

Function	Return type	Function	Return type
CBool	**Boolean**	**CInt**	**Integer**
CByte	**Byte**	**CLng**	**Long**
CCur	**Currency**	**CSng**	**Single**
CDate	**Date**	**CVar**	**Variant**
CDbl	**Double**	**CStr**	**String**
CDec	**Decimal**		

The code below shows the use of a few of these functions which make it explicit what type of calculation is being carried out.

```
one = 10
two = 3
StringResult$ = CStr(one) + CStr(two)      ' gives 103
IntegerResult% = CInt(one) + CInt(two)     'gives 13
IntegerAverage% = CInt(one) / CInt(two)    ' gives 3
SingleAverage! = CSng(one) / CSng(two)     ' gives 3.3333
```

Rounding and truncating integers

The **CInt** and **CLng** functions always round to the nearest number, for example 3.9 rounds to 4 while 5.2 rounds to 5. There is often some confusion between these functions and the **Int** and **Fix** functions, both of which truncate a number, for example 7.9 is truncated to 7.

The difference between **Int** and **Fix** is in the way in which they deal with negative numbers: **Int** will convert to the first negative integer less than or equal to the number, while **Fix** produces the first integer greater than or equal to the number, for example -7.9 produces -8, while **Fix** will truncate -7.9 to -7.

Arithmetic operators

We have looked at a few of the operators which Visual Basic uses for arithmetic. The complete list is shown in table 6.4.

Table 6.4 *The arithmetic operators.*

Operator	Action	Example
+	Addition.	$3 + 7 = 11$
-	Subtraction.	$8 - 2 = 6$
*	Multiplication.	$2.1 * 4 = 8.4$
/	Division.	$21 / 2 = 10.5$
^	Exponentiation.	$3 ^ 2 = 9$
\	Integer division.	$6 \setminus 1.6 = 3$
Mod	Modulus, returns the remainder after integer division.	8 **Mod** $3 = 2$

Arrays

Arrays are used to collect together pieces of data which are of the same type: for example a list of people's names could be stored as an array of type **String**, a list of exam marks could be stored as an array of type **Integer**. Arrays can have more than one dimension, for example a timetable could be stored as a two–dimensional array.

Declaring arrays

Before an array can be used it must be declared using the **Dim** statement.

Dim name (subscripts) [As type] [, ...]

The simplest arrays have only one dimension, for example:

Dim ListOfNames(5) As String

This defines a one–dimensional array with six elements: *ListOfNames(0)* to *ListOfNames(5)*. The statement:

Dim *ListOfNames(0* **To** *5)* **As String**

is equivalent.

If a lower bound is not explicitly stated, the lower limit is zero. The following are all equivalent:

Dim *IntList(7, 2)* **As Integer**
Dim *IntList(0* **To** *7, 0* **To** *2)* **As Integer**
Dim *IntList(7, 0* **To** *2)* **As Integer**

It is important to choose a style that you like and to stick with it for consistency.

You can choose up to sixty dimensions for an array.

A static array has its dimensions declared within the **Dim** statement, a dynamic array has its dimensions declared at run–time with a **ReDim** statement.

Changing array dimensions

Visual Basic allows you to create dynamic arrays, that is arrays whose dimensions have not been declared, and to specify the dimensions at run–time using the **ReDim** statement, for example:

Dim *Range( )* **As Integer**   *' declare a dynamic array*
......
ReDim *Range(0* **To** *300)*   *' give the dynamic array some dimensions*

The **ReDim** statement changes the number of elements so that the first is 0 and the last is 300.

You can use the **ReDim** statement repeatedly to change the size of the array at run–time.

The type of an array cannot be changed unless it is a **Variant** array, in which case it can be changed to a specified type by adding an **As** *type* clause to the **ReDim** statement.

If you want to preserve values already in the array, you need to use the optional keyword **Preserve**, otherwise they are erased.

Dim *Range( )* **As Integer**
ReDim *Range (10* **To** *20)*
... ...
... ...
ReDim Preserve *Range (10* **To** *30)*

This will retain the values stored in the array, but there are some limitations: you can only resize the last array dimension and you cannot change the number of array elements. If you reduce the number of elements in the array rather than increasing it, data will be lost.

The Erase statement

If you want to free the memory space taken up by a dynamic array , you can use the **Erase** statement, for example:

> *Dim MyArray(10 to 20) As Integer*
> *... ...*
> *Erase MyArray*

For static arrays the space is not recovered. Instead **Erase** sets the elements of the array to "empty" values.

- For numeric arrays, **Erase** sets each element to zero.
- For **String** static arrays, **Erase** sets each element to an empty string ("").

User–defined data types

Visual Basic allows you to group related pieces of data together: for example if you want to save information on a collection of computers in an office, including the processor type, the memory size and cost, you can create a data type which groups this information together and then define an array of this type. The information we want to save is shown in table 6.5. Each row represents our new data type.

Table 6.5 User–defined data types.

Processor	MemorySize	Cost
Pentium III 600	256	2000
Pentium Celeron 400	128	900
Pentium 150	64	300

Each row of the table can be grouped together in a user–defined data type defined by the **Type** statement, which must be placed in the General section of a standard module, that is not within a module which processes event procedures originating from a form.

> *Type Specification*
> *Processor As **String***
> *MemorySize As **Integer***
> *Cost As **Currency***
> *End Type*

To create a standard module select the **Project I New Module** menu option, display the **New** page and select the **Module** option. Add the type definition to the General section by selecting **(General)** from the list on the top left of module's code window and typing the definition.

You can define an array of this type in the same way as an array of standard Visual Basic types is defined, for example:

> *Dim Computer(5) As Specification*

You can refer to all of the data items in the array, for example, to change the first row of the array:

Computer(0).Processor ="Pentium III 600"
Computer(0).MemorySize = 128
Computer(0).Cost = 2000

7
Using Menus

Introduction

Virtually every Windows application has a menu system underneath the title bar. Many features of menus in a Windows application are standard: the first menu item is always *File* and this offers options which allow you to open, close and save files; the last menu item is always *Help*. This helps to give all Windows applications a family feel and makes it easier to learn new applications.

In this chapter we are going to look at how to create menus using a powerful and yet intuitive Menu Editor and see how to respond to events which occur when a menu item is selected.

The Menu Editor

To run the Menu Editor click on the icon on the tool bar, shown in figure 7.1, or press **Ctrl+E** or select the **Tools | Menu Editor** menu item.

Figure 7.1 *The Menu Editor icon*

The Menu Editor is shown in figure 7.2. The first heading on the menu system we are going to create has a **Caption** of *File*. It must have a unique **Name** property so that we can refer to it unambiguously in our application. It is a common convention to start the name of menu items with the prefix *mnu*, so the name of this entry is *mnuFile*. It is usual in Windows applications to be able to specify a menu item by using a combination of the **Alt** key and one of the letters in the menu item name – in the case of this item, we want to be able to select this entry by pressing **Alt+F**. We do this by placing the & character in front of the letter F in the **Caption**, so the caption becomes

&File. The & character does not appear on the menu. When you have entered the **Caption** and **Name** click on the **Next** button.

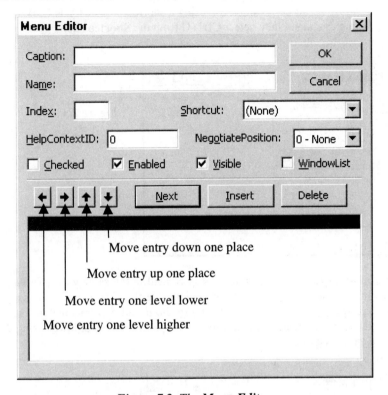

Figure 7.2 The Menu Editor.

Do not worry if you make a mistake when entering a menu item, since it is easy to change items and to move their position, using the four arrowed keys in the Menu Editor. The buttons with the vertical arrows move the position of a selected item. The buttons with the two horizontal arrows change the level of the item selected. Since the *File* entry we have just made appears on the menu bar it is at the highest level. Menu entries which appear when you click on *File* are at the next lower level.

We are going to add the menu items which are on the next level below the *File* menu item to produce the menu shown in figure 7.3.

To add these menu items below the *File* menu:

- Set the **Caption** property to *& Open*, so that it can be executed by pressing **Alt+O**.
- Set the **Name** property to *mnuOpen*.
- Click on the button with the horizontal right facing arrow to move it down a level, so that it appears below *File* when the application runs and not on the menu bar.
- Set the **Caption** property of the next entry to –, this will display a solid line.
- Set the **Name** property to *mnuDash1*, every solid line must have a unique name.

- Add the **Save** and **Save As** menu items and a solid line in the same way. Note that the caption for the **Save As** entry will be **Save &As**.
- The *Close* menu item can be run using a shortcut key of **Ctrl+C**. When you are entering this menu item select **Ctrl+C** from the **Shortcut** list.

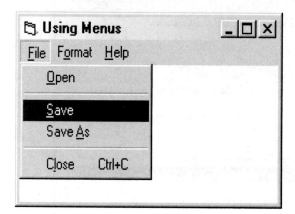

Figure 7.3 *The File menu.*

The *Format* menu shown in figure 7.4 is created in the same way. *Format* is at the top level and so appears on the menu bar alongside the *File* menu. *Font* is at a lower level and appears below *Format*. The *Italic*, *Bold* and *Size* menu items are inserted directly below *Font* in the **Menu Editor** and are placed one level lower using the button with the right facing arrow.

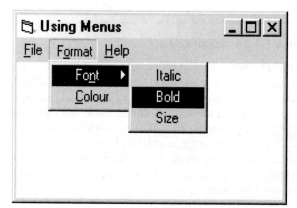

Figure 7.4 *The Format menu.*

The **Menu Editor** showing the completed menu is shown in figure 7.5.

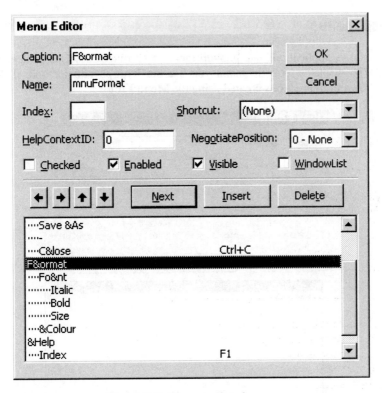

Figure 7.5 The completed menu.

Enabling and disabling controls

Sometimes menu controls need to be disabled, for example, the *Paste* command in an editor if nothing has been cut or copied beforehand. All the menu commands have an **Enabled** check box. If this is set to **False** the menu control appears in light grey and does not respond to clicking. The run–time command is of the form:

*ControlName.**Enabled** = False*

If a menu title is disabled all the menu items below it are automatically disabled. Menu controls can also be disabled by making them invisible:

*ControlName.**Visible** = False*

If there are other menu items on the title bar a gap is not left where the invisible menu item had been: the menu items on the right of the menu item shift left to fill the gap.

Pop–up menus

Most Windows applications use pop–up menus to provide a set of context sensitive options. To display a pop–up menu you use the **PopupMenu** method, if the menu system shown in figure 7.6 is created using the **Menu Editor**.

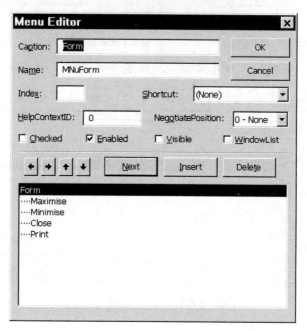

Figure 7.6 Creating a pop–up menu.

The *Form* menu item is called *MnuForm* and has four sub–items. Since this is to be a pop–up menu item its **Visible** property must be set to **False** when the form is loaded so that it is not displayed on the menu bar:

> **Private Sub** *Form_Load( )*
> *MnuForm.Visible = False*
> **End Sub**

The **Visible** property of the items, *Maximise, Minimise, Close* and *Print*, must remain as **True**.

If you want to add additional pop–up menus you can do so in the same way. If you want menu items to remain on the menu bar, leave their **Visible** property to the default value of **True**.

To display the form when the right mouse button is clicked the MouseDown event handler for the form must test to see if the right button has been clicked and then call the **PopupMenu** method:

> *Private **Sub** Form_MouseDown(Button **As Integer**, Shift **As Integer**,*
> *X **As Single**, Y **As Single**)*

> *If Button = 2 **Then PopupMenu** MnuForm*
> **End Sub**

The pop–up menu displayed is shown in figure 7.7.

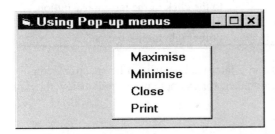

Figure 7.7 The pop–up menu.

In the example shown only the single mandatory parameter, the name of the menu, is given, but there are a further four optional parameters. The full syntax for this method is:

> *object.PopupMenu menuName, flags, x, y, boldCommand*

*Table 7.1 The **PopupMenu** method.*

Parameter	Comments
object	Optional. If omitted, the menu applies to the form which has the focus.
menuName	Required. The name of the pop–up menu. The menu specified must have at least one sub–menu.
flags	Optional. A value which specifies the location and behaviour of the menu. This is described below.
x	Optional. The x co–ordinate of the menu. If omitted the x mouse position is used.
y	Optional. The y co–ordinate of the menu. If omitted the y mouse position is used.
boldCommand	Optional. The name of a menu control to display in bold. If omitted none are bold.

The values for the flags parameter are in two parts which describe both the location and behaviour:

Table 7.2 The location values for the flags parameter.

Constant	Value	Description
vbPopupMenuLeftAlign	0	The left of the menu is at the x position.
vbPopupMenuCenterAlign	4	The centre is at x.
vbPopupMenuRightAlign	8	The right is at x.

Table 7.3 *The behaviour values for the flags parameter.*

Constant	Value	Description
vbPopupMenuLeftButton	0	The selected item on the menu reacts to the click of the left mouse button.
vbPopupMenuRightButton	2	The selected item reacts to the click of the right mouse button.

If optional parameters are omitted and a later parameter is to be specified, commas must be used to specify the missing parameter, for example in the code below the *flags* parameter is omitted.

> *Form1.MnuForm , , 200, 300*

To use the *flags* parameter it is clearer if you use the constants, for example:

> *Form1.MnuForm,* ***vbPopupMenuLeftAlign*** *+* ***vbPopupMenuRightButton****, 50,200*

The x and y co–ordinates are relative to top left corner of form which displays the menu.

Menu events

The menus we have created so far have not had any events associated with them. The simplest way to create an event procedure for a menu item is to click on the menu item you want to write the event procedure for; and the template procedure is created for you; for example, the outline event procedure for the *Save As* menu option is shown:

> ***Private Sub*** *mnuSaveAs_Click( )*
> ......
> ***End Sub***

In conformity with the Visual Basic standards, the procedure name is made up of the **Name** of the menu item, *mnuSaveAs*, an underscore character and the name of the event, *Click*.

You can also create outline event procedures by firstly selecting the name of the menu item, from the list of controls and menu items on the top left of the project code window and secondly selecting the event from list of events on the top right of that window.

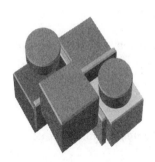

8

Forms and Dialogs

Introduction

Dialog boxes are a special type of window which are used for either displaying information, or in some cases asking for information. You can create your own custom dialog boxes, but there are also a set of standard dialogs for operations that applications frequently use, for example there is a standard dialog which is used for opening a file. It is no accident that every Windows application displays the same format of dialog box when carrying out these types of action.

The MsgBox statement and function

The **MsgBox** statement and function are both used to display a dialog box. The difference between them is that the **MsgBox** function returns an integer value, which indicates which button on the dialog has been clicked. If there is only one button on the dialog you can use the **MsgBox** statement, since you are not interested in the returned value.

The **MsgBox** function creates and displays a message box. It has five parameters, but only the first one is mandatory:

intValue = MsgBox(prompt, buttons, title, helpfile, context)

The **MsgBox** statement has the same set of parameters but a very slightly different syntax:

MsgBox *prompt, buttons, title, helpfile, context*

In its simplest form, **MsgBox** it has only one parameter, the text which it displays. If, for example, you create an application which has a single button, with the default name, and add the following code to its click event procedure as shown:

```
Private Sub Command1_Click( )
    Dim ButtonPressed As Integer
    ButtonPressed = MsgBox("Click OK to finish")
End Sub
```

the dialog shown in figure 8.1 is displayed. It has an **OK** button. The title text is the application name.

Figure 8.1 The simplest dialog box.

In this case there is only one button on the dialog, so it would be better to use the **MsgBox** statement:

> *MsgBox "Click OK to finish"*

This displays exactly the same dialog, and we do not need to create an integer variable which receives the return value returned by the **MsgBox** function.

The text can be up to 1024 characters long. If you want to spread it over more than one line you can include carriage return or line feed characters in the text string, for example:

```
Private Sub Command1_Click( )
    Dim text As String
    text = "You can build up very long lines, up to 1024 characters" & Chr(13)
    text = text + "and specify explicit line breaks by using" & Chr(13)
    text = text + "the Chr function.  Chr(13) is a line feed"
    MsgBox text, , "A long dialog"
End Sub
```

This produces the dialog shown in figure 8.2.

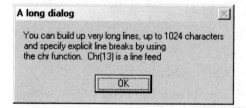

Figure 8.2 Displaying multiple lines.

Note that the second parameter which determines the buttons displayed on the dialog has not been included, so only the default **OK** button is displayed; but the third parameter, which is the title which is added to the top of the dialog, is included.

The button parameter

The button parameter is more complicated than it initially seems and is used to specify the following features:

- The combination of buttons displayed.
- The default button.
- The icon displayed on the dialog.
- The modality of the dialog.
- The text alignment.
- Whether the text is displayed in left–to–right or right–to–left format which is used in Hebrew and Arabic systems.

Visual Basic has a set of constants for each of these features which can be combined to give the dialog format you want.

There are seven combinations of buttons which can be displayed as shown in table 8.1:

Table 8.1 *Button constants for dialogs.*

Value	Constant	Buttons displayed
0	**vbOKOnly**	**OK** button only.
1	**vbOKCancel**	**OK** and **Cancel** buttons.
2	**vbAbortRetryIgnore**	**Abort**, **Retry** and **Ignore** buttons.
3	**vbYesNoCancel**	**Yes, No** and **Cancel** buttons.
4	**vbYesNo**	**Yes** and **No** buttons.
5	**vbRetryCancel**	**Retry** and **Cancel** buttons.
16384	**vbMsgBoxHelpButton**	**Help** button.

You can control which of the buttons displayed is the default button, as shown in table 8.2:

Table 8.2 *Default button constants for dialogs.*

Value	Constant	The default button
0	**vbDefaultButton1**	The first, leftmost button.
256	**vbDefaultButton2**	The second.
512	**vbDefaultButton3**	The third.
768	**vbDefaultButton4**	The fourth.

There are four possible icons shown in table 8.3:

Table 8.3 *Icon constants for dialogs.*

Value	Constant	Icon	Value	Constant	Icon
16	vbCritical		32	vbQuestion	
48	vbExclamation		64	vbInformation	

Dialogs created by the **MsgBox** function, and as we shall see later, by the **InputBox** function are application modal. This means that you must respond to the dialog, so that it is closed. You cannot move to another part of the application until you have done so. You can, however, move to another application. You can also make these dialogs system modal, which means that not only can the current application not proceed until the dialog is closed, but no other application can continue either. The default is application modal; system modality is only used in situations where you are prompting for a log–on password and want to prevent access to the computer unless a correct password is supplied.

Table 8.4 *Modality constants for dialogs.*

Value	Constant	Buttons displayed
0	vbApplicationModal	The dialog is application modal.
4096	vbSystemModal	The dialog is system modal.

If you create a form in Visual Basic this is by default non–modal and you can leave it open and continue with the application or switch to another application.

Since these constants are integers they can be added together to form a single button parameter, for example:

```
Private Sub Command1_Click( )
    MsgBox "Error writing to file", vbDefaultButton1 + _
    vbAbortRetryIgnore + vbSystemModal + vbCritical, _
    "Disk write error"
End Sub
```

Note the use of the continuation character _ at the end of the first two lines. This produces the dialog shown in figure 8.3.

It shows the text *Error writing to file*, the first button is the default, it displays the **Abort Retry** and **Ignore** buttons, it is system modal and shows the critical icon. The caption on the dialog is *Disk write error*.

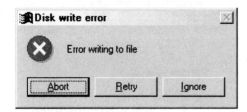

Figure 8.3 *Specifying dialog features.*

The helpfile and context parameters

The final two parameters in the **MsgBox** function are the *helpfile* string and a *context* value. You must specify both of these parameters or neither of them. The *helpfile* parameter identifies the Help file used to supply context–sensitive Help for the dialog box. The *context* value identifies the Help topic within the Help file.

Using returned values

The dialogs which we have seen so far have simply displayed information and a selection of buttons. If we use the **MsgBox** function rather than the **MsgBox** statement we can also find out which button has been pressed and take appropriate action. There are seven possible values which can be returned, one for each of the buttons which may be displayed, listed in table 8.5.

Table 8.5 *Returned values of the MsgBox function.*

Value	Constant	Buttons pressed
1	vbOK	OK
2	vbCancel	Cancel
3	vbAbort	Abort
4	vbRetry	Retry
5	vbIgnore	Ignore
6	vbYes	Yes
7	vbNo	No

If the dialog contains a **Cancel** button, pressing the **Escape** key has the same effect as pressing that button.

The code below displays a dialog with two buttons, **OK** and **Cancel**; if the **OK** button is pressed a second dialog asking if you are really sure is displayed. The two dialogs are shown in figure 8.4.

```
Private Sub Command1_Click( )
    Dim format As Integer, confirmation As Integer
    format = MsgBox("Format operation will erase all data", _
    vbOKCancel + vbExclamation, "Format")
```

*If format = **vbOK Then** confirmation = **MsgBox**("Are you sure ?", _*
*   **vbYesNo** + **vbInformation**, "Format Warning!")*
*   **End Sub***

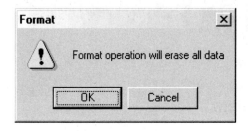

Figure 8.4 *Detecting which button has been pressed.*

Dialogs can also be used to input text, but to do this we have to use the **InputBox** function.

The InputBox function

The **InputBox** function behaves in a similar way to the **MsgBox** function. Dialogs created with **InputBox** do not display an icon and have **OK** and **Cancel** buttons, however, you can specify the position of the dialog.

stringValue = **InputBox**(*prompt, title, default, xpos, ypos, helpfile, context*)

- The returned value *stringValue* contains the string typed in the dialog.
- The *prompt* is a mandatory parameter which is displayed on the dialog.
- The *title* is the title displayed on the title bar of the dialog.
- The *default* parameter specifies the text which will returned by the function if no other input is made.
- *xpos* and *ypos* are the x and y position in twips of the top left corner from the top left corner of the screen. If these values are not supplied the dialog is positioned in the centre of the screen.
- The *helpfile* and *context* provide a connection to a context–sensitive Help file.

All of the parameters are optional apart from *prompt*. If you click on the **OK** button or press **Enter**, the text typed is returned in *stringValue*. If the **Cancel** button is clicked or the **Escape** key is pressed a zero–length string is returned.

The code below creates the dialog shown in figure 8.5.

```
Private Sub Command1_Click( )
   Dim destination As String
   Do
         destination = InputBox("Enter destination", "Vacation destinations", _
         "Hawaii", 100, 300)
         If destination <> "" Then MsgBox "You have chosen " & destination
```

> **Loop Until** *destination* <> " "
> **End Sub**

The dialog displaying the default text of *Hawaii* has been replaced with a new holiday destination. If you click on the **Cancel** button, the dialog is displayed again, since *destination*, the string returned, will be empty. If you enter a holiday destination in the TextBox and click **OK**, another dialog is displayed.

*Figure 8.5 Using the **InputBox** function.*

The dialog is displayed with its top left corner at position 100, 300.

The CommonDialog control

All windows applications have a similar appearance – for example whenever you open or save a file, choose a colour, or print a document – since Windows has a set of standard dialog boxes which carry out these operations. You can incorporate them into your applications by using the CommonDialog control. If this control is not available in your Toolbox, you need to add it from the **Project | Components** menu option and selecting the **Microsoft CommonDialog Control 6.0** option.

Figure 8.6 The CommonDialog control.

It does not matter where you place the CommonDialog control, shown in figure 8.6, on your design forms since it is invisible at run–time, and you will see only the dialog box which you want to use.

The CommonDialog control can display six different types of standard dialog, each of which is displayed by a different method.

- File Open ~ displayed by the **ShowOpen** method.
- File Save As ~ displayed by the **ShowSave** method.
- Colour selection ~ displayed by the **ShowColor** method.
- Font selection ~ displayed by the **ShowFont** method.
- Printer selection ~ displayed by the **ShowPrinter** method.
- Invokes the Windows Help engine ~ displayed by the **ShowHelp** method.

There is a different method for displaying each of these dialogs

The File Open dialog

The File Open dialog, shown in figure 8.7 allows you to browse through your file system and to select one or more files. It is virtually identical to the File Save dialog apart from its title.

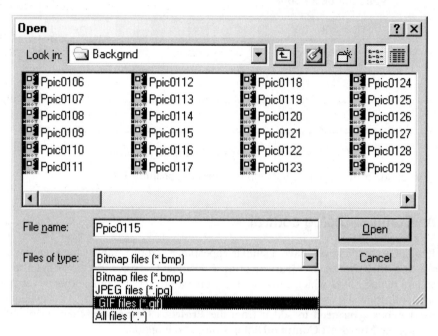

Figure 8.7 *The Open File dialog.*

Figure 8.7 was produced by starting a new project and adding a CommandButton renamed to *UsingCommonDialog*, a CommonDialog control renamed to *OpenFile,* and an Image control. The code shown below shows the click event procedure for the button:

```
Private Sub UseCommonDialog_Click( )
    OpenFile.InitDir = "D:\"
    OpenFile.Filter = "Bitmap files (*.bmp)|*.bmp|" & _
    "JPEG files (*.jpg)|*.jpg|" & _
    "GIF files (*.gif)|*.gif|" & _
    "All files (*.*)|*.*"
    OpenFile.ShowOpen
    Image1.Picture = LoadPicture(OpenFile.FileName)
End Sub
```

The dialog is assigned an initial folder using the **InitDir** property. By default the dialog will show all of the files in the current folder, but you can limit this to files of a specified extension by using the **Filter** property. This property has a number of parts to it. The first part, *Bitmap files (*.bmp)* specifies the text which is displayed in the **Files of type** text box. The next part delimited by the I character specifies the type of files to be displayed. If you want to display an alternative set of files you need to use the & character and then specify the new file type in the same way. Unusually for Visual Basic the syntax seems fussy, in particular it is essential not to leave any spaces between the I characters and other characters. In figure 8.7 you can choose between displaying bmp, jpg, gif or all files.

The dialog is displayed by the **ShowOpen** method. The file name which is selected is returned in the **Filename** property. In this example it is passed to the **LoadPicture** method and displayed in an Image control.

Since the CommonDialog can display a wide variety of dialogs, it has properties which are not always useful, for example the **Color** property indicates the colour selected from the Color dialog box and does not make any sense if you want to display a File Open dialog. Some of the most commonly–used properties of the CommonDialog control when a File Open or File Save dialog are displayed are shown in table 8.6.

Table 8.6 *Key properties of the CommonDialog displaying a File Open/Save dialog.*

Property	Description
DefaultExt	The file extension specified in this property is automatically applied when a file name is typed.
FileName	This is either the default file name which appears when the dialog is displayed or the name of the file selected.
FileTitle	The name of the file without its path.
Filter	Specifies the types of files which are displayed by the dialog on the basis of their extension.
FilterIndex	The default filter for the dialog.
Flags	This property is used to select certain features of the dialog such as whether a file is read only, it is covered next in this chapter
InitDir	Sets the initial directory for the dialog. It is often useful to assign this to **App.Path**, that is the current directory of the **App** object. **App** is the global object which retains information on the current application.

The **Flags** property sets some features of the dialog which is displayed. Visual Basic has nearly twenty different values which can be assigned to this property in different combinations, for example:

*OpenFile.**Flags** = cdlOFNFFileMustExist*

specifies that the files which you select must already exist. Some of the most common values for the **Flags** property are shown in table 8.7.

Table 8.7 *Key constants for the **Flags** property for Open/Save dialogs.*

Property	Description
cdlOFNAllowMultiSelect	Allows multiple selection of files.
cdlOFNExplorer	Displays the dialog in an Explorer type format.
cdlOFNLongNames	Allows long file names
cdlOFNFileMustExist	The file entered must exist, if an invalid file name is entered a warning is displayed.
cdlOFNHelpButton	A Help button is displayed on the dialog.
cdlOFReadOnly	The **Read Only** check box is initially checked, but you can choose to override it.

If you decide to allow multiple file selection and add the line:

OpenFile.Flags = cdlOFNAllowMultiSelect

to the application before the **ShowOpen** method is executed, the dialog is displayed in a slightly different format as shown in figure 8.8. You can select more than one file from the list in the usual way, by pressing the **Ctrl** key to select a new file without de-selecting other files or by using the **Shift** key to select all the files between the current file and another selected file either above or below it.

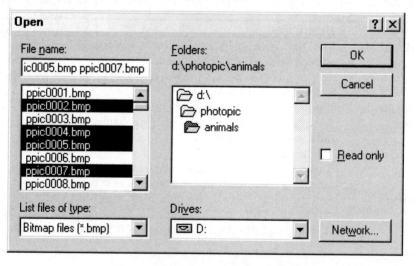

Figure 8.8 *Selecting multiple files.*

The **Filename** property returns the path and then the names of all the files selected. In figure 8.8 four files have been selected and the returned text is:

D:\photopic\animals ppic0002.bmp ppic0004.bmp ppic0005.bmp ppic0007.bmp

It is easy to extract the individual file names by looking for a space, but if you are using long file names which include a space there is a problem since you cannot tell which spaces are a part of the name and which mark the end of the file name. To solve this problem if you want multiple file selection also set the **Flag** property to accept long file names (**cdlOLongNames**) and to use the Explorer style dialog (**cdlOFNExplorer**), this uses the **Chr(0)** character to separate the file names.

The Color dialog

The Color dialog, shown in figure 8.9, allows you to choose a colour; it is returned in the **Color** property.

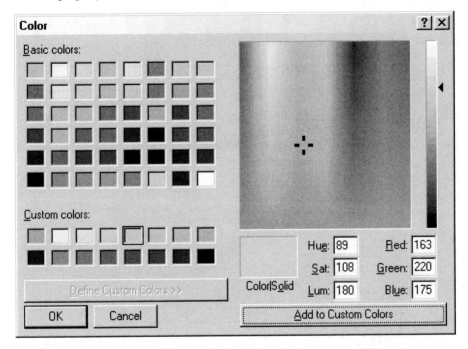

Figure 8.9 *The Color dialog.*

To display this dialog, create a new application and add a single button and a CommonDialog control. Change the name of the button to *ChangeColor* and the name of the CommonDialog to *ColorDialog*. The code below shows the Click event procedure for the button.

```
Private Sub ChangeColor_Click( )
    ColorDialog.Flags = cdlCCFullOpen
    ColorDialog.ShowColor
    Form1.BackColor = ColorDialog.Color
End Sub
```

The **Flags** property has been assigned the value **cdlCCFullOpen**, this is not strictly necessary in this case since the default is to display the full form of the dialog including the right side of the dialog which allows you to select custom colours. If you do not want your application to offer this facility you can set the **Flags** property to

cdlCCPreventFullOpen. The **ShowColor** method displays the dialog and the colour selected is returned in the **Color** property which is used to change the background colour of the form to the colour selected.

The Font dialog

The Font dialog, shown in figure 8.10, allows you to choose the style of font you want.

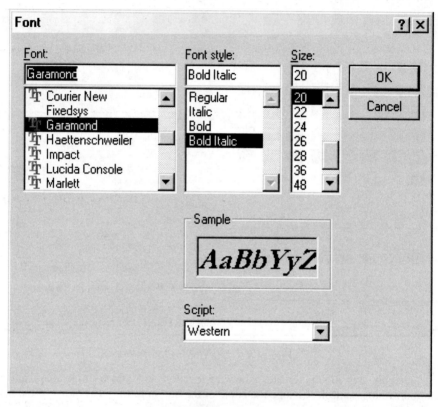

Figure 8.10 *The Font dialog.*

The different aspects of the font, its name, size and whether it is bold or italic, are returned in separate properties. To display the Font dialog shown in figure 8.10, create an application with a text box, renamed *Chameleon*, a CommandButton renamed *ChangeFont* and a Common Dialog control renamed *FontDialog*. The font characteristics of the text in the text box, called *Chameleon*, are changed to the values selected in the Font dialog.

The code below is the click event procedure for the CommandButton.

```
Private Sub ChangeFont_Click( )
    FontDialog.Flags = cdlCFScreenFonts        ' screen fonts only
    FontDialog.ShowFont
```

> *Chameleon.Font.Bold = FontDialog.FontBold*
> *Chameleon.Font.Italic = FontDialog.FontItalic*
> *Chameleon.Font.Name = FontDialog.FontName*
> *Chameleon.Font.Size = FontDialog.FontSize*
> **End Sub**

The **Flags** property is set to display only the screen fonts available (**cdlCFScreenFonts**); alternatively you can set it to display the printer fonts only using the **cdlCFPrinterFonts** constant or both using **cdlCFBoth**. The dialog is displayed using the **ShowFont** method. Each of the returned font aspects are assigned to the corresponding aspect of the **Font** property of the text box.

The most commonly–used values for the **Flags** property for Font dialogs are shown in table 8.8.

Table 8.8 *Key constants for the **Flags** property for Font dialog.*

Constant	Description
cdlCFANSIOnly	Displays only fonts that use the Windows character set.
cdlCFBoth	Displays both screen and printer fonts.
cdlCFEffects	Allows strikethrough, underline and colour effects to be selected.
cdlCFLimitSize	Only allows the selection of fonts between the **Min** and **Max** properties.
cdlCFPrinterFonts	Displays the printer fonts only.
cdlCFScalableOnly	Only allows scalable fonts to be selected.
cdlCFScreenFonts	Displays only screen fonts.
cdlCFTTOnly	Displays only TrueType fonts.
cdlCFWYSIWYG	Displays only fonts which are available on both the screen and the printer. If this option is chosen, also set the **cdlCFBoth** and **cdlCFScalableOnly** flags.

The Print dialog

The Print dialog, shown in figure 8.11, allows you to specify details of the information you want to print. To display this dialog a CommonDialog called *PrintDialog* and a CommandButton called *ShowPrint* were added to a form. The event procedure for the CommandButton is shown below:

> **Private Sub** *ShowPrint_Click( )*
> *PrintDialog.**ShowPrinter***
> **End Sub**

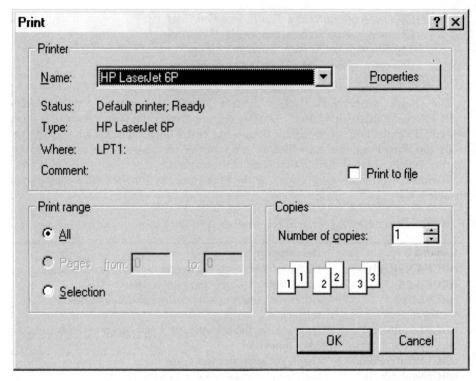

Figure 8.11 The Print dialog.

There are numerous flags for the Print dialog, the most commonly–used ones are shown in table 8.9.

***Table 8.9** Key constants for the **Flags** property for Print dialog.*

Constants	Description
cdlPDAllPages	Sets the state of the **All Pages** button.
cdlPDCollate	Sets the state of the **Collate** check box.
cdlPDHidePrintToFile	Disables the **Print To File** check box.
cdlPDPrintSetup	Displays the **Print Setup** dialog rather than the Print dialog.
cdlPDPrintToFile	Sets the **Print To File** check box.

If the **Flags** property is set to **cdlPDPrintSetup**, the Print Setup dialog shown in figure 8.12 is displayed.

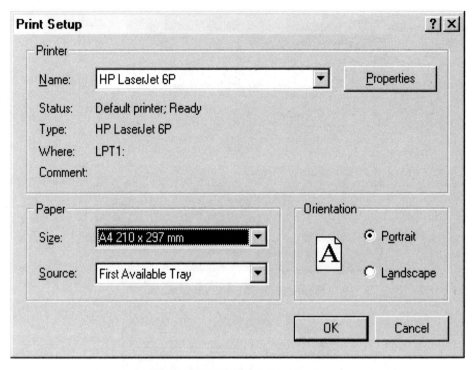

Figure 8.12 The Print Setup dialog.

Creating custom dialogs

The dialogs which the CommonDialog control displays are an essential part of virtually every application and you do not need to customise them.   Visual Basic also has a number of dialogs where a common format tends to be used in different applications, but where there is some scope for you to amend a standard format to the exact form you want, for example when creating a *Tip of the Day* dialog or an *About* dialog. To see the types of dialog which you can add to your project select the **Project** I **Add Form** menu option to display the Add Form dialog which is shown in figure 8.13.

If you want to use one of dialogs available, select it and click on the **Open** button to add it to your application. The idea of these dialogs is that you use them as the basis of the dialog that you want. A few of the dialogs available are shown in figures 8.14 to 8.16.

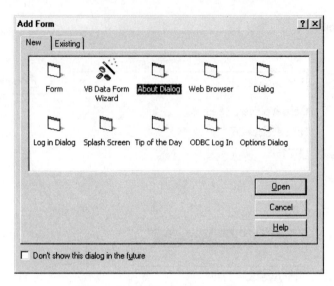

Figure 8.13 *The Add Form dialog.*

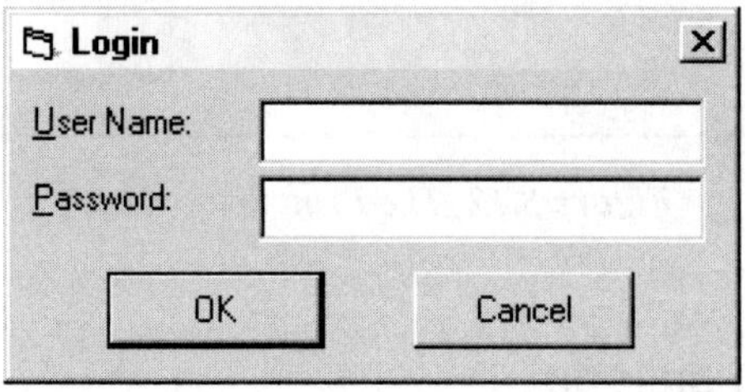

Figure 8.14 *The Login dialog.*

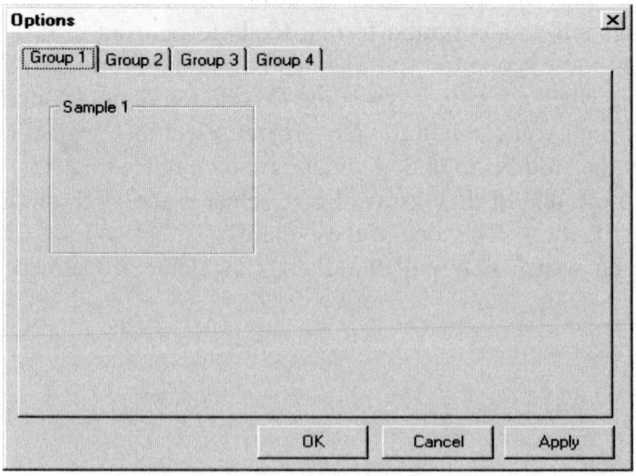

Figure 8.15 *The Options dialog.*

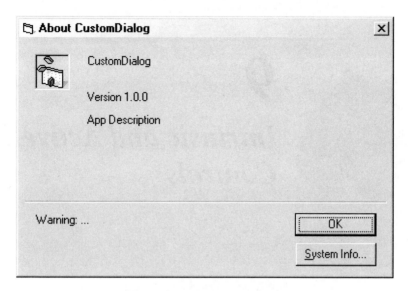

Figure 8.18 The About dialog.

Showing and hiding dialogs

To display any form or dialog use the **Show** method, for example to display a form called *AboutDialog*:

> *AboutDialog.Show*

The **Load** statement copies the dialog into memory but does not display it, for example:

> **Load** *AboutDialog*

If you use the **Load** statement when the application starts, perhaps when a splash screen is displayed, when the **Show** method is used it will operate much faster since the form it is to display is already in memory.

To hide a dialog (but not remove it from memory) use the **Hide** method.

> *AboutDialog.Hide*

To hide and remove a dialog from memory use the **UnLoad** statement, for example:

> **Unload** *AboutDialog*

If you want to specify that a form is the first to be displayed when the application runs, as is likely to be the case with the Login dialog, select the **Project | Properties** menu option and specify the name of the form you want to display first in the **Startup Object** list.

9

Intrinsic and ActiveX Controls

Introduction

One of the great features of Visual Basic is that it has an excellent set of standard controls and a huge number of additional controls, some supplied by Microsoft and many supplied by other companies. It is a good idea to use existing controls wherever possible: if they come from a well–known company they have been thoroughly tested and will help you to develop applications with as few bugs as possible in the shortest time.

In this chapter we are going to look at some of the intrinsic controls we have not used yet and some of the most commonly–used ActiveX controls.

The Timer control

The Timer control shown in figure 9.1 is one of the intrinsic Visual Basic controls. It allows you to trigger an event at regular intervals. In the application we are going to look at, this Timer control is used for updating a clock. It does not matter where you place the Timer control since it is not visible at run–time.

Figure 9.1 *The Timer control.*

- To display an updated clock a Label control is used to display the time. The name of the **Caption** is changed to *Clock*.
- Add a Timer control to the application and set the **Enabled** property to **True**.

- Set the **Interval** property of the Timer to the length of the time between the Timer events in milliseconds, 1000 in this case so the clock display is updated every second.
- In the Timer event for the Timer, set the **Caption** property of the Label to the current time using the **Time** function:

Private Sub *Timer1_Timer( )*
   *Clock.***Caption** = *Time*
End Sub

The ListBox control

The ListBox control, shown in figure 9.2, has very similar behaviour to the ComboBox control, but a different appearance.

Figure 9.2 The ListBox control icon.

To see how this control is used we are going to develop the application shown running in figure 9.3. The ListBox control displays a lists of sports which are added to the list at run–time. You can select one or more of the sports: as you do so, the sports you have selected are displayed in the TextBox control at the bottom of the form. You can add a new sport to the list by typing it into the TextBox on the right of the form and clicking the *Add a new sport* button. You can delete one or more selected sports by clicking on the *Delete selected sports* button.

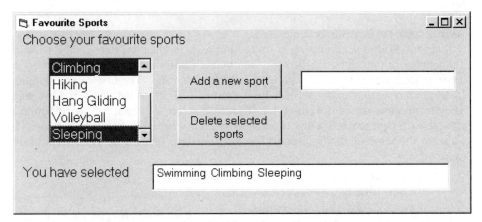

Figure 9.3 Using the ListBox control.

To create this application:

- Create a user interface similar to figure 9.3.
- Change the name of the ListBox to *Sports*.

- Change the name of the two buttons to *AddSport* and *RemoveSport*.
- Change the name of the TextBox where the new sports are typed to *NewSport*.
- Change the name of the TextBox which displays the selected sports to *SportList*.
- To ensure that more than one item can be selected from the ListBox set the **MultiSelect** property to **Simple**.
- Set the **Text** properties of the two TextBox controls to "", so that no text is displayed when the application starts.
- You can add items to a ListBox design–time using the **List** property, but in this application we are adding the items at run–time using the **AddItem** method in the Form Load event:

```
Private Sub Form_Load( )
    Sports.AddItem "Soccer"
    Sports.AddItem "Swimming"
    Sports.AddItem "Ice Hockey"
    Sports.AddItem "Climbing"
    Sports.AddItem "Hiking"
    Sports.AddItem "Hang Gliding"
    Sports.AddItem "Volleyball"
    Sports.AddItem "Sleeping"
End Sub
```

To add the sport typed into the *NewSport* TextBox to the ListBox when the *AddSport* button is pressed:

```
Private Sub AddSport_Click( )
    Sports.AddItem NewSport.Text
    NewSport.Text = ""
End Sub
```

The text in the TextBox is also erased.

Since the **MultiSelect** property is set to **Simple**, more than one item can be selected. The number of items in a ListBox is given by the **ListCount** property. Each entry in the ListBox is stored in the **List** property, which is an array. The first item is stored in **List**(0) and if there is only one item **ListCount** is 1. Each of the items in a list has a **Selected** property which is **True** if that list item is selected. When the *Sports* button is clicked, each item in the ListBox is checked to see if it has been selected. If it has, it is added to the selected sports displayed in the *SportList* TextBox at the bottom of the form.

```
Private Sub Sports_Click( )
    SportList.Text = ""
    For c = 0 To Sports.ListCount - 1
        If Sports.Selected(c) = True Then _
        SportList.Text = SportList.Text & " " & Sports.List(c) & " "
    Next c
End Sub
```

Finally, to activate the delete button, each list item in turn is checked to see if it is selected, if it is, the item is deleted. There is one complication: in the *Sports_Click* event procedure above, the loop starts at zero and ends on *Sports.**ListCount** - 1*, the last item in the list; however, whenever we delete an item from the list using the **RemoveItem** method, the value of **ListCount** decreases by one, since an item has been deleted from the list. This causes the application to crash if we have the same **For..Next** loop. The solution is to start the loop at the last entry in the list and then move backwards down the list, looking at the last entry in the list first. The **Step** of the **For..Next** loop is -1.

> **Private Sub** *RemoveSport_Click( )*
>   **For** *c = Sports.**ListCount** - 1* **To** *0* **Step** *-1*
>   **If** *Sports.**Selected**(c) = **True Then** _*
>   *Sports.**RemoveItem** c*
>   **Next** *c*
>   *SportList.**Text** = ""*
> **End Sub**

Some of the most commonly–used properties of the ListBox control are shown in table 9.1.

Table 9.1 *Key properties of the ListBox control.*

Property	Description
Columns	The number of list items displayed on a line. The default is 1.
List	An array which contains the items in the list. **List**(0) is the first item.
ListCount	The number of items in the list.
ListIndex	The number of the list item selected, 0 for the first item. Always one less than the maximum value of **ListCount**. If no item is selected it is -1.
MultiSelect	If **None**, only one item can be selected. If **Simple**, items are selected by clicking the mouse or pressing the spacebar. If **Extended**, pressing **Shift** and either clicking the mouse or pressing an up or down arrow key extends the selection from a previously selected item. Pressing **Ctrl** and clicking the mouse selects or deselects an item.
Selected	A boolean array, **True** if the list item is selected.
Sorted	If **True** the list items are displayed in alphabetical order.
Style	Either **Standard** or **Checkbox** if you wish to display a CheckBox adjacent to each list item.

Most of these properties and the methods we have looked at are shared with the ComboBox.

The Slider control

The Slider control, shown in figure 9.4, is used to change a value by moving the position of the slider bar along a track.

Figure 9.4 *The Slider control icon.*

In the example we are going to look at, the value of the red, green and blue components of the colour of the TextBox control are controlled by moving three sliders as shown in figure 9.5. The current value of each slider is shown by the Label control on the right of each of the Slider controls. When you move the cursor over the slider bar its current value is displayed in a small pop–up message as shown for the *Blue* slider.

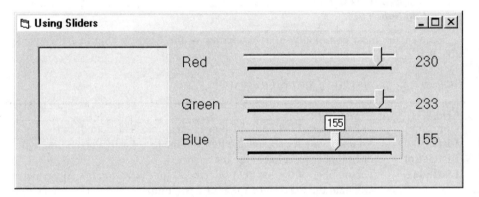

Figure 9.5 *Using the Slider control to specify colours.*

To create this application:

- Select the **Project** | **Components** menu option.
- Add the **Microsoft Windows Common Controls 6.0** (MSCOMCTL.OCX) to the application.
- Create the user interface so that it is similar to figure 9.5.
- Change the name of the three sliders to *Red*, *Green* and *Blue*.
- Change the name of the three Labels adjacent to the Slider controls to *RedValue*, *GreenValue* and *BlueValue*.
- Change the name of the TextBox control to *ColorChooser*.

The position of the slider bar is shown by the **Value** property of the control. You can control the range of values using the **Min** and **Max** properties. **Min** is the value returned when the slider bar is at the far left of its range and **Max** is returned when it is at the far right. Set **Min** to 0 and **Max** to 255 for all of the Slider controls, since the range of the value for the red, green and blue components of a colour is within this range.

The user interface is now complete and the values of the relevant design–time properties set, but we need to write some Visual Basic code to make the application function. We need to initialise the application:

- Assign initial values for the Slider controls.
- Assign the corresponding values shown in the Label controls adjacent to each Slider.
- Assign the colour of the TextBox to the colour specified by the *Red*, *Green* and *Blue* Slider controls.

The best place to initialise the application is in the Form Load event procedure:

```
Private Sub Form_Load( )
    Red.Value = 122:        RedValue.Caption = Red.Value
    Blue.Value = 122:       BlueValue.Caption = Blue.Value
    Green.Value = 122:      GreenValue.Caption = Green.Value
    ColorChooser.BackColor = RGB(Red.Value, Green.Value, Blue.Value)
End Sub
```

The **RGB** function takes the red, green and blue values of the colour as integer values between 0 and 255, an **RGB**(0, 0, 0) corresponds to black and **RGB**(255, 255, 255) corresponds to white. Note the use of the colon character : to allow two Visual Basic statements to be placed on one line.

In the Click event procedure for the *Red* Slider controls we need to use the **RGB** function to set the colour of the TextBox to correspond to the values of the Slider controls (including the changed Red Slider control) and to update the Label, *RedValue*:

```
Private Sub Red_Click( )
    ColorChooser.BackColor = RGB(Red.Value, Green.Value, Blue.Value)
    RedValue.Caption = Red.Value
End Sub
```

The event procedures for the *Green* and *Blue* sliders are very similar:

```
Private Sub Green_Click( )
    ColorChooser.BackColor = RGB(Red.Value, Green.Value, Blue.Value)
    GreenValue.Caption = Green.Value
End Sub
Private Sub Blue_Click( )
    ColorChooser.BackColor = RGB(Red.Value, Green.Value, Blue.Value)
    BlueValue.Caption = Blue.Value
End Sub
```

Some of most commonly–used properties of the Slider control are shown in table 9.2.

Table 9.2 *Key properties of the Slider control.*

Property	Description
SelectRange	If **True** a range of values can be selected.
SelStart	The start of the selection range. The value must be greater than the value of the **Min** property.
SelLength	The length of the selected range. **SelStart + Length** must be less than the value of the **Max** property.
SmallChange	The change in the value returned by the Slider when the bar is moved.
LargeChange	The change in the value returned by the Slider when the slider track is clicked.
Max	The maximum value returned by the Slider.
Min	The minimum value returned by the Slider.
TickFrequency	The distance between the tick marks placed on the slider track.
TextPosition	Two possible values: **sldAboveLeft** positions the ToolTipText on the left of the slider for vertical sliders and above for horizontal sliders; **sldBelowRight** positions the text below or to the right of the slider.
ToolTipText	The text displayed when the cursor pauses over the Slider control.
Value	The value returned by the Slider which indicates the position of the Slider bar.

The RichTextBox control

The RichTextBox control is an extended version of the TextBox control: unlike the TextBox it can display text in variety of sizes, fonts and sizes. In a TextBox the **Font** property applies to all the text which it displays. The RichTextBox control has a number of properties which control text formatting, but these only apply to selected text. The RichTextBox control does not have a 64K limit on the amount of text it can control as the TextBox does. In common with the TextBox control it is a data–bound control and can be connected to a text field in a database.

To use this control, shown in figure 9.6, you need to add the control to your Toolbox by selecting the **Project | Properties** menu option and choosing the **Microsoft Rich TextBox 6.0** option (RICHTX32.OCX).

Figure 9.6 The RichTextBox control.

The application which we are going to develop to see this control in action is shown in figure 9.7. Clicking on the *Find File* button opens the File Open dialog and allows you to choose an RTF file to open. The *Font* button displays the Font dialog and allows you to change the font characteristics of selected text only.

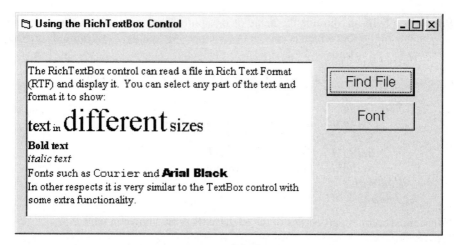

Figure 9.7 Using the RichTextBox control.

To create the application:

- Start a new project and add the RichTextBox control to the project Toolbox.
- Add a RichTextBox control to the form and change its name to *DisplayText*.
- Add two buttons to the form.
- Change the **Caption** on one button to *Find File* and change its **Name** to *GetFileName*.
- Change the **Caption** of the second button to *Font* and change its **Name** to *ChangeFont*.
- Add two CommonDialog controls to the form. Change the **Name** of one to *GetFile*, change the name of the other to *FontDialog*.

This completes the user interface. The next stage is to add the code behind the two buttons. When the *GetFileName* button is clicked, the Open File dialog is displayed. An initial directory is set using the **InitDir** property and the **Filter** property is used so that only RTF files or all files are displayed in the dialog, although the RichTextBox control can display text from ASCII text files as well. When a file has been selected its name is returned in the **FileName** property. The file name is passed to the **LoadFile** method of the RichTextBox called *DisplayText* to display the text read from the file in the RichTextBox. To write to a file the corresponding **SaveFile** method is used.

```
Private Sub GetFileName_Click( )
    GetFile.InitDir = "C:\Books\VB\v6.0\richTextBox"
    GetFile.Filter = "RTF files (*.rtf)|*.rtf|" & "All files (*.*)|*.*"
    GetFile.ShowOpen
    DisplayText.LoadFile (GetFile.FileName)
End Sub
```

The *ChangeFont* button displays the Show Font dialog. The **Flags** property is used to specify that only screen fonts are to be made available. The name of the font selected, its size and whether the font is bold or italic is returned and assigned to the corresponding properties of the selected text in the RichTextBox. For example,

DisplayText.**SelFontName** is the name of the font of the selected text, this is assigned to the name of the font which is chosen in the Open File dialog, *FontDialog*.**FontName**.

```
Private Sub ChangeFont_Click( )
    FontDialog.Flags = cdlCFScreenFonts      ' screen fonts only
    FontDialog.ShowFont
    With DisplayText
        .SelFontName = FontDialog.FontName
        .SelFontSize = FontDialog.FontSize
        .SelBold = FontDialog.FontBold
        .SelItalic = FontDialog.FontItalic
    End With
End Sub
```

The most common properties of the RichTextBox are shown in table 9.3.

Table 9.3 Key properties of the RichTextBox control.

Property	Description
SelBold	If **True** the selected text is bold.
SelColor	Changes the colour of selected text.
SelFontName	The name of the font.
SelFontSize	The size of the characters.
SelItalic	If **True** the selected text is italic.
SelStrikethru	If **True** the selected text is struck through.
SelUnderline	If **True** the selected text is underlined.
SelRTF	The currently–selected text in the RichTextBox.
TextRTF	The entire contents of the RichTextBox.

The MonthView control

Many applications need to display a calendar and to allow a date or a range of dates to be selected. The MonthView control shown in figure 9.8 is a useful ActiveX control which displays, in its simplest form, a month at a time.

To add this control to your Toolbox select the **Project | Components** menu item and select the **Microsoft Windows Common Controls–2 6.0** option (MSCOMCT2.OCX) to the application.

Figure 9.8 The MonthView control icon.

The control in action is shown in figure 9.9. The current date is circled and there are a range of options to allow you to select a range of dates. You can move to show the months before or after using the arrowed keys at the top of the control.

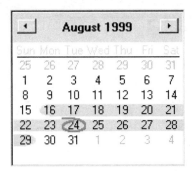

Figure 9.9 *The MonthView control.*

The most commonly–used properties of this control are shown in table 9.4.

Table 9.4 *Key properties of the MonthView control.*

Property	Description
MonthColumns	Specifies the number of months displayed horizontally. The default is 1.
MonthRows	Specifies the number of months displayed vertically.
MultiSelect	Set to **True** if more than one date can be selected.
MaxSelCount	Specifies the maximum number of days which can be selected if **MultiSelect** is **True**.
SelStart	The first date in selected dates.
SelEnd	The last date in the selected dates.
ShowToday	Set to **True** to display the current date at the bottom of the current month.
ShowWeekNumber	If **True** the number of weeks since the start of the year are displayed.
Week	The number of weeks since the start of the year.

When you click on a date the **DateClick** event occurs, whenever a new date is selected the **SelChange** event occurs.

The DateTimePicker control

The icon for this control, shown in figure 9.10, is included in the MSCOMCT2.OCX file with the MonthView control.

Figure 9.10 *The DateTimePicker control icon.*

The DateTimePicker (DTPicker) control is very flexible and allows you to display dates and times in a wide variety of formats, you can even add your own formats if you wish. Figure 9.11 shows DateTimePicker controls with a variety of property settings.

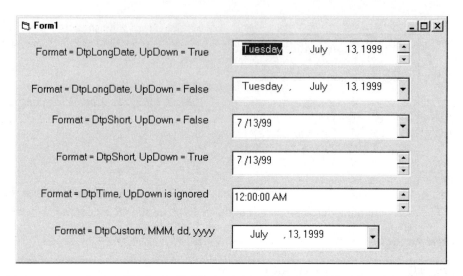

Figure 9.11 Using the DTPicker control.

The most common design–time properties of this control are shown in table 9.5.

Table 9.5 Key design–time properties of the DateTimePicker control.

Property	Description
Format	Four possible values: **dtpLongDate**, **dtpShortDate**, **dtpTime** and **dtpCustom**. The effects of these can be seen in figure 9.11.
UpDown	If a date and time are displayed and this property is **False**, clicking on the down arrow displays the MonthView control for date selection. If **UpDown** is **True**, selecting any part of the date allows you to increment or decrement it.
CustomFormat	If the format property is **dtpCustom**, this property specifies the custom format of the date and time.
MinDate	The earliest possible date.
MaxDate	The latest possible date.
Value	The date as displayed.

If the **Format** property is assigned the value **dtpCustom** you can create your own format of dates and times, for example a **CustomFormat** value of *MMM, dd, yyyy* will display the full month name, the day of the month and the year as a four digit number, for example July, 13, 1999. You can specify any date format that you wish, for a complete list of the formatting characters look at the **CustomFormat** property in the Visual Basic Help.

There are five properties which control allow you to control all aspects of the colour of the DateTimePicker control: **CalendarBackColor**, **CalendarTitleBackColor** **CalendarForeColor**, **CalendarTitleForeColor** and **CalendarTrailingForeColor** properties

If you wish you can extract the date and time from the **Value** property, however, there is a useful group of run–time properties which allow you to access individual parts of the date and time as shown in table 9.6.

Table 9.6 *Key run–time properties of the DateTimePicker control.*

Property	Description
Second	An integer between 0 and 59.
Minute	An integer between 0 and 59.
Hour	An integer between 0 and 23.
Day	An integer between 1 and 31.
DayOfWeek	An integer between 1(Sunday) and 7(Saturday). It is better to use the constants **mvwSunday**, **mvwMonday** and so on, rather than the numbers.
Month	An integer between 1 and 12. If you wish you can use the constants **mvwJanuary**, **mvwFebruary** and so on.
Year	An integer giving the year.

The MSFlexGrid control

The MSFlexGrid control is used for displaying tabular information, both text and pictures; you can even display text and pictures in the same cell. To include this control, shown in figure 9.12, on your Toolbox use the **Projects | Components** menu option and include the **Microsoft FlexGrid Control 6.0** option (MSFLXGRD.OCX).

Figure 9.12 *The MSFlexGrid control icon.*

This control is flexible and has an extensive range of features, and although it is not particularly complex, it is not a straightforward control to use. Unlike most Visual Basic controls the names of many of the properties are not clear, for example the **Rows** property is the number of rows in the grid, while the **Row** property is the number of the current row. It is easy to make mistakes with these property names. A major limitation is that it is not possible to enter data into the grid at design–time, which is often inconvenient. The biggest limitation is that you cannot edit the contents of a cell directly. If you want to simulate in–cell editing you have to place a TextBox control over the cell you want to edit and to adjust the size, position and content of the TextBox so that it exactly matches the cell. It is not a difficult procedure but you do have to write quite a lot of Visual Basic code to carry out an operation which you will often need in applications.

Some of the essential properties of this control are shown in table 9.7.

Table 9.7 *Key design–time properties of the MSFlexGrid control.*

Property	Description
Col	The column of the current cell.
Row	The row of the current cell.
Cols	The number of columns.
Rows	The number of rows.
ColWidth	The width of the specified column.
RowHeight	The height of the specified row.
WordWrap	If **True** and the text on a cell will not fit on to a single line it will wrap on to the next line.
FixedCols	The number of fixed columns.
FixedRows	The number of fixed rows.
Width	The width of the entire control.
Height	The height of the whole control.
CellPicture	The picture displayed in the current cell.
Text	The text displayed in a single cell.
CellLeft	The distance of the left edge of the current cell from the left of the control.
CellTop	The distance of the top of the current cell from the top of the control.
CellHeight	The height of the current cell.
CellWidth	The width of the current cell.
GridLineWidth	The width of the grid lines.
AllowUserResizing	This controls whether the columns and rows of the control can be resized at run–time. It can be one of four values: **FlexResizeNone**, **FlexResizeColumns**, **FlexResizeRows** or **FlexResizeBoth**.
ColSel	Marks the start or end of a column of cells, the other end of the selection is given by **Col** (the column of the current cell). When combined with **ColRow** an area of cells can be selected.
ColRow	Marks the start or end of a row of cells, the other end of the selection is given by **Row** (the row of the current cell).

Using the MSFlexGrid control

To see how these properties are used in practice and in particular to see how we can simulate in–cell editing we are going to develop an application which displays a set of Visual Basic icons in a grid and allows us to edit the text. The running application is shown in figure 9.13. Note that this application has one fixed row and one fixed column of cells, that is the **FixedCols** and **FixedRows** properties are both 1. The fixed cells appear grey and are not available for editing.

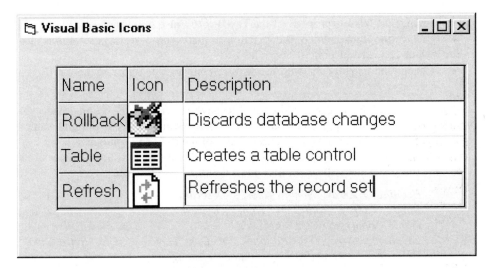

Figure 9.13 The application at run–time.

To create this application:

- Add a MSFlexGrid control and a TextBox control to the form as shown in figure 9.14. The position of the TextBox does not matter since the TextBox is not visible when the application first runs and it later overlays a grid cell.

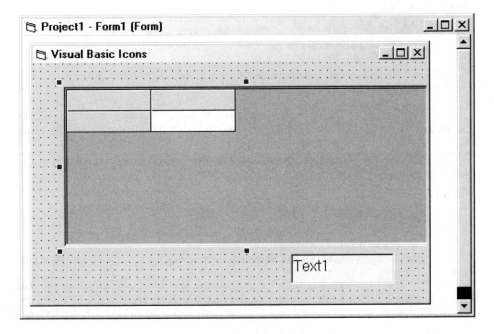

Figure 9.14 The application at design–time.

- Change the **Visible** property of the TextBox to **False** so it is not seen.
- Change the **BackColor** of the TextBox so that when it overlays a cell it is clear which cell is being edited.
- Change the name of the MSFlexGrid to *Icons* and the name of the TextBox to *Overlay*.

The first Visual Basic event procedure we have to write is the Form Load event which occurs when the application starts. This is a common place to put information into the MSFlexGrid control and to setup the size of the rows and columns.

Four arrays are created containing the title at the top of the control, the names of the icons, the full pathname of the icon files and a description of the icons:

> *Headings = **Array**("Name", "Icon", "Description")*
> *Names = **Array**("Rollback", "Table", "Refresh")*
> *D = "C:\books\vb\v6.0\UsingGrids\"*   *' the file location*
> *Locations = **Array**(D & "Rollback.ico", D & "Table.ico", D & "Refresh.ico")*
> *Description = **Array**("Discards database changes", _*
> *   "Creates a table control", _*
> *   "Refreshes the record set")*

The **Rows** and **Cols** property gives the number of rows and columns in the control, the **Height** property gives the overall height of the control:

> *Icons.**Rows** = 4*
> *Icons.**Cols** = 3*
> *Icons.**Height** = 0*
> *'set the heights of the rows and the overall height of the control*
> **For** *r = 0* **To** *Icons.**Rows** - 1*
> *   Icons.**RowHeight**(r) = 500*
> *   Icons.**Height** = Icons.**Height** + Icons.**RowHeight**(r) + 20*
> **Next** *r*

The height of all of the rows is 500 twips and the overall height of the control is calculated by adding the row heights together plus a small amount for the size of the border.

The width of the columns is setup and the **Width** property, which gives the overall width of the control, is calculated.

> *' set the widths of the columns and the overall width of the control*
> *Icons.**ColWidth**(0) = 1000*
> *Icons.**ColWidth**(1) = 800*
> *Icons.**ColWidth**(2) = 4000*
> *Icons.**Width**=Icons.**ColWidth**(0)+Icons.**ColWidth**(1)+Icons.**ColWidth**(2)+90*

The text and icons are added to the grid a row at a time. When using the **Text** property to find or set the text in a cell, the cell which is referenced is given by the value of the **Row** and **Col** properties which identifies the current cell. The **CellPicture** property is used to assign a graphic to the cells.

```
' add the text to the Headings
    Icons.Row = 0
    For c = 0 To Icons.Cols - 1
        Icons.Col = c
        Icons.Text = Headings(c)
    Next c
'set the rows of information, row 1 first then row 2 and so on
    For r = 1 To Icons.Rows - 1
        Icons.Row = r
        Icons.Col = 0
        Icons.Text = Names(r - 1)
        Icons.Col = 1
        Set Icons.CellPicture = LoadPicture(Locations(r - 1))
        Icons.Col = 2
        Icons.Text = Description(r - 1)
    Next r
```

The next event procedure we need to write is when a key is clicked in any cell. This procedure has to fit the TextBox exactly on top of the cell where the key was pressed, so that it appears that the cell itself is being edited.

```
Private Sub Icons_KeyPress(KeyAscii As Integer)
' the text in the text field is the text in the cell & the key pressed
    Overlay.Text = Icons.Text & Chr(KeyAscii)
' set the size and position of the TextBox to overlay the cell
    Overlay.Left = Icons.CellLeft + Icons.Left
    Overlay.Top = Icons.CellTop + Icons.Top
    Overlay.Width = Icons.CellWidth
    Overlay.Height = Icons.CellHeight
```

The text in TextBox called *Overlay*, is set to be the same as the text in the cell where the key has been pressed. The **Left** property of the TextBox is assigned to the distance of the left side of the current cell from the left edge of the MSFlexGrid control plus the distance of the left of the grid from the side of the form. A similar process is carried out to setup the **Top** property of the TextBox. The width and height of the TextBox are set to be the same as the width and height of the cell. When this has been done the TextBox should exactly overlay the cell.

The TextBox is now made visible and the **SelStart** property is used to move the cursor to the end of the text. This property gives the start of selected text, or if no text is selected the current cursor position. The **Len** function gives the length of the text. The last line in this event procedure gives the focus to the TextBox.

```
' make the TextBox visible
    Overlay.Visible = True
' position the cursor at the end of the text in the TextBox
    Overlay.SelStart = Len(Overlay.Text)
' assign the TextBox the focus
    Overlay.SetFocus
```

The final event procedure updates the text in the selected cell, so that the text in the TextBox and the text in the cell are the same.

> ***Private Sub*** *Overlay_Change( )*
> *' update the grid cell*
>   *Icons.**Text** = Overlay.**Text***
> ***End Sub***

The complete listing of this application is shown below. The MSFlexGrid has a poor performance which becomes noticeable when managing a large number of cells and coupled with the other limitations in its functionality and the confusing property names makes this one of the least satisfactory Visual Basic controls.

> ***Private Sub*** *Form_Load( )*
>   *Headings = **Array**("Name", "Icon", "Description")*
>   *Names = **Array**("Rollback", "Table", "Refresh")*
>   *D = "C:\books\vb\v6.0\UsingGrids\" ' the file location*
>   *Locations = **Array**(D & "Rollback.ico", D & "Table.ico", D & "Refresh.ico")*
>   *Description = **Array**("Discards database changes", _*
>   "Creates a table control", _*
>   "Refreshes the record set")*
>   *Icons.**Rows** = 4*
>   *Icons.**Cols** = 3*
>   *Icons.**Height** = 0*
> *'set the heights of the rows and the overall height of the control*
>   ***For** r = 0 **To** Icons.**Rows** - 1*
>   *Icons.**RowHeight**(r) = 500*
>   *Icons.**Height** = Icons.**Height** + Icons.**RowHeight**(r) + 20*
>   ***Next** r*
> *' set the widths of the columns and the overall width of the control*
>   *Icons.**ColWidth**(0) = 1000*
>   *Icons.**ColWidth**(1) = 800*
>   *Icons.**ColWidth**(2) = 4000*
>   *Icons.**Width**=Icons.**ColWidth**(0)+Icons.**ColWidth**(1)+Icons.**ColWidth**(2)+90*
> *' add the text to the Headings*
>   *Icons.**Row** = 0*
>   ***For** c = 0 **To** Icons.**Cols** - 1*
>   *Icons.**Col** = c*
>   *Icons.**Text** = Headings(c)*
>   ***Next** c*
> *'set the rows of information, row 1 first then row 2 and so on*
>   ***For** r = 1 **To** Icons.**Rows** - 1*
>   *Icons.**Row** = r*
>   *Icons.**Col** = 0*
>   *Icons.**Text** = Names(r - 1)*
>   *Icons.**Col** = 1*
>   ***Set** Icons.**CellPicture** = **LoadPicture**(Locations(r - 1))*
>   *Icons.**Col** = 2*

```
        Icons.Text = Description(r - 1)
    Next r
End Sub
Private Sub Icons_KeyPress(KeyAscii As Integer)
' the text in the text field is the text in the cell & the key pressed
    Overlay.Text = Icons.Text & Chr(KeyAscii)
' set the size and position of the TextBox to overlay the cell
    Overlay.Left = Icons.CellLeft + Icons.Left
    Overlay.Top = Icons.CellTop + Icons.Top
    Overlay.Width = Icons.CellWidth
    Overlay.Height = Icons.CellHeight
' make the TextBox visible
    Overlay.Visible = True
' position the cursor at the end of the text in the TextBox
    Overlay.SelStart = Len(Overlay.Text)
' assign the TextBox the focus
    Overlay.SetFocus
End Sub
Private Sub Overlay_Change( )
' update the grid cell
    Icons.Text = Overlay.Text
End Sub
```

The UpDown control

The icon for the UpDown control shown in figure 9.15 is a simple but very useful
control which allows you to increment or decrement a value in another control.

          Figure 9.15 *The UpDown control icon.*

To add this control to your Toolbox select the **Project | Components** menu item and
select the **Microsoft Windows Common Controls–2 6.0** option (MSCOMCT2.OCX)
to the application.

The key properties of the control are shown in table 9.8.

In the application shown running in figure 9.16 there are two TextBox controls and
two UpDown controls. Note that the TextBox on the left contains an integer value and
does not require any Visual Basic code, but the TextBox on the right contains a date and
a few lines do need to be written.

Table 9.8 *Key properties of the UpDown control.*

Property	Description
BuddyControl	The name of the control which is linked to the UpDown control.
BuddyProperty	The name of the property in the buddy control which is incremented or decremented by the UpDown control.
SyncBuddy	Set to **True** to establish the link between the UpDown control and the buddy.
Increment	The amount by which the property is changed when an up or down arrow is clicked.
Min	The lower limit.
Max	The upper limit.
Orientation	Either **cc2OrientationVertical** or **cc2OrientationHorizontal** to display the arrows vertically or horizontally.
Value	The current value of the property.

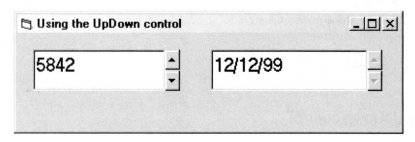

Figure 9.16 *Using the UpDown control.*

To write this application:

- Add two TextBox controls and two UpDown controls to the form.
- Change the names of the TextBox controls to *TheValue* and *TheDate*.
- Change the name of the UpDown controls to *ChangeTheValue* and *ChangeTheDate*.
- Change the **BuddyControl** property of *ChangeTheValue* to *TheValue* to link the TextBox and the UpDown control.
- Change the **BuddyProperty** of *ChangeTheValue* to **Text**, to link the **Text** property of the TextBox to the UpDown control.
- Change the **Max** property of *ChangeTheValue* to 1000 and the **Min** property to 0.
- Change the **BuddyControl** property of *ChangeTheDate* to *TheDate* to link the TextBox and the UpDown control.
- Change the **BuddyProperty** of *ChangeTheDate* to **Text**.
- Change the **Max** and **Min** properties of *ChangeTheDate* to 0, since the control this UpDown control is linked to is a date.

If you run the application now you will find that the TextBox with the integer values can be incremented and decremented correctly, but to change the TextBox with the date we need to write some Visual Basic code.

You can set the initial date at design–time or in the Form Load event:

```
Private Sub Form_Load( )
    TheDate.Text = #12/12/1999#
End Sub
```

When the down arrow on an UpDown control is clicked a DownClick event occurs. In this event procedure we need to check that the field, *TheDate*.**Text**, we wish to decrement is a valid date, using the **isDate** function. If it is the **CDate** function converts the field to a date and it is then decremented. *TheDate*.**Text** is then made equal to the new date. The code for doing this is shown below:

```
Private Sub ChangeTheDate_DownClick( )
    If IsDate(TheDate.Text) Then _
    TheDate.Text = CDate(TheDate.Text) - ChangeTheDate.Increment
End Sub
```

A similar few lines of code handle the UpClick event except that the date is incremented.

```
Private Sub ChangeTheDate_UpClick( )
    If IsDate(TheDate.Text) Then _
    TheDate.Text = CDate(TheDate.Text) + ChangeTheDate.Increment
End Sub
```

The ProgressBar control

The ProgressBar has a rectangle which is filled from left to right as an application proceeds. It is a useful control when your application is carrying out an operation which takes a long time. It is very frustrating if you are using an application which you think may have locked up, but you are not sure. If there is a ProgressBar control which shows that the application is progressing it is very reassuring.

This control is included in MSCOMCTL.OCX with the Slider control. To add this file to your application select the **Project | Components** menu option and select **Microsoft Windows Common Controls 6.0.**

The most commonly–used properties of the ProgressBar control are shown in table 9.9.

The application we are going to develop to see this control in action is shown in figure 9.17. An integer is entered into the central TextBox and when the Button is clicked a check is made to see if it is a prime number or not. The result is displayed in the right TextBox.

Table 9.9 *Key properties of the ProgressBar control.*

Property	Description
Max	The value when the ProgressBar is filled.
Min	The value when the ProgressBar is empty.
Scrolling	The way in which the ProgressBar is filled can be either **ccScrollingStandard**, which fills the rectangle in separate blocks, or **ccScrollingSmooth**. which fills it with one continuous band.
Value	The current value of the ProgressBar.

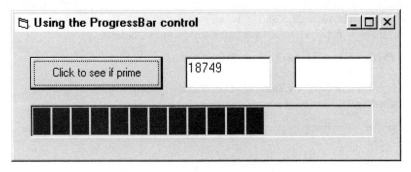

Figure 9.17 *Using the ProgressBar control.*

If you enter a six–digit number, the calculation can take a long time, so the ProgressBar has been added to provide an indication that the application is working and has not crashed. In this application a very unsophisticated method is used to calculate if a number is prime. The number is divided by all of the numbers between 2 and half of the number specified. The minimum value of the ProgressBar is therefore 2 and the maximum value is assigned to the number of times the loop is executed. Every time the loop is executed the **Value** property of the ProgressBar is incremented. The ProgressBar works out from this the number of blocks to display.

The **Name** property of the ProgressBar has been changed to *PBar*. The name of the TextBox where the number is entered is called *Test* and the other TextBox which displays a message indicating if the number is prime or not is called *theResult*. When the button, called *CheckPrime*, is clicked its event procedure is run:

```
Private Sub CheckPrime_Click( )
' if you can exactly divide a number by any other number apart from
' 1 and itself to give a remainder of zero the number is not a prime number
    PBar.Min = 2
    PBar.Value = PBar.Min
    PBar.Max = CLng(Test.Text / 2)
    Prime = True
    For c = Start To Test.Text / 2
        If (Test.Text Mod c = 0) Then Prime = False
        If PBar.Value <> PBar.Max Then PBar.Value = PBar.Value + 1
    Next c
```

> **If** *Prime* **Then** *TheResult.***Text** *= "Prime"* **Else** *TheResult.***Text** *= "Not prime"*
> **End Sub**

When the calculation is complete and the number in the *Test* TextBox is changed, its Change event procedure is executed and the message indicating whether the value is prime or not is erased.

> ***Private Sub*** *Test_Change( )*
>   *TheResult.***Text** *= ""*
> ***End Sub***

10

Mouse and Keyboard Events

Introduction

We have looked at many events associated with controls such as clicking on a button or selecting an item from a list. Windows applications support a set of events which occur when a key on the keyboard is clicked and when the mouse is moved or one of its button is clicked. In this chapter we are going to look at these events and also how they can be used to handle the dragging and dropping of a control.

The KeyPress event

When an ANSI key is pressed the KeyPress event occurs. The object which has the focus receives the event. This may be a control such as a TextBox or a form. The KeyPress event occurs before the key pressed is displayed, so you have an opportunity to change it.

The event procedure for this event when a TextBox with the default name of *Text1* has the focus starts:

> *Private Sub Text1_KeyPress(KeyAscii As Integer)*

You can convert the integer passed to the event procedure into a character using the **Chr** function, for example

> *myChar = Chr(KeyAscii)*

If you change the value of *myChar*, you can use the **Asc** function which converts from a character to an integer, to change *KeyAscii*, for example:

> *KeyAscii = Asc(myChar)*

The new value of *KeyAscii* is the character which is displayed as a result of the key press.

If you want to refer to a key such as the **Delete** key there is a complete set of constants which represent each key in the Visual Basic Help under key code constants listed in the Help index under **key code constants**.

One of the uses of this event is to ensure that only certain characters may be entered, for example in figure 10.1, only numeric digits and the delete character (key code **vbKeyBack**) are echoed. For any other character *KeyAscii* is assigned the value zero which cancels the keystroke.

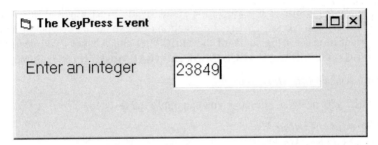

Figure 10.1 The KeyPress event.

The KeyPress event procedure for the text box is shown below:

```
Private Sub Text1_KeyPress(KeyAscii As Integer)
    If Not IsNumeric(Chr(KeyAscii)) And KeyAscii <> vbKeyBack _
    Then KeyAscii = 0
End Sub
```

The KeyUp and KeyDown events

When an ANSI key is pressed the KeyUp and KeyDown events occur in addition to the KeyPress events. This pair of events also occur when keys other than the ANSI keys are pressed, for example, for:

- The function keys.
- The navigation keys.
- Key combinations, for example **Shift+A**.

These events do not occur in three situations:

- The **Enter** button is pressed and the form has a button which has its **Default** property set to **True**.
- The **Escape** key is pressed and the form has its **Cancel** property set to **True**.
- The **Tab** key is pressed.

The header for the event procedure for a form when the KeyDown event occurs is shown below:

*Private Sub Form_KeyDown(KeyCode As **Integer**, Shift As **Integer**)*

The KeyUp event procedure has the same pair of parameters, unlike the KeyPress event which only has one parameter. The *KeyCode* indicates the key pressed, for example **vbKeyF1** if the **F1** key is pressed, and the *Shift* parameter indicates the status of the **Shift**, **Ctrl** and **Alt** keys.

Using bit masks

Bit 0 of the *Shift* parameter represents the status of the **Shift** key and bits 1 and 2 the status of the **Ctrl** and **Alt** keys. Any combination of these three keys can be set.

If you want to test for the status of the **Shift**, **Ctrl** and **Alt** keys you need to use the three bit masks, **vbShiftMask**, **vbCtrlMask** and **vbAltMask**. If for example:

*Shift And **vbShiftMask** > 0*

then the **Shift** was pressed, similarly you can apply the tests:

*Shift And **vbCtrlMask** > 0*
*shift And **vbAltMask** > 0*

to see if the **Ctrl** and **Alt** keys were pressed.

Using the KeyUp and KeyDown events

In the next application, shown running in figure 10.2, the graphic, which is stored in an Image control called *Arrows*, can be moved around the form using the four arrowed keys. The **Picture** property of the Image control also changes depending on which arrowed key is pressed, for example a left pointing arrow if the left arrow key is pressed. If you try this application, you need to create graphics of the four arrows using any drawing package and specify their location in the Form Load event handler.

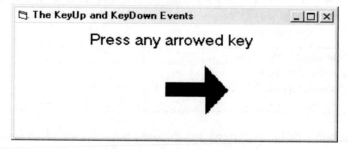

Figure 10.2 *The KeyUp and KeyDown events.*

When the form is loaded the directory is changed to the directory containing the four graphics files:

```
Private Sub Form_Load( )
    ChDir ("C:\books\vb\v6.0\keyupdown")        ' specify where your own file are
End Sub
```

If the KeyDown event occurs a check is made to see if the up arrow navigation key has been pressed. If so, the corresponding up arrow graphic file is loaded and the **Top** property of the Image control is decreased by 10. This process is repeated to check for the other arrowed navigation keys. The complete code is shown below:

```
Private Sub Form_KeyDown(KeyCode As Integer, Shift As Integer)
    If KeyCode = vbKeyUp Then
        Arrows.Picture = LoadPicture("UpArrow.bmp")
        Arrows.Top = Arrows.Top - 10
    End If
    If KeyCode = vbKeyDown Then
        Arrows.Top = Arrows.Top + 10
        Arrows.Picture = LoadPicture("DownArrow.bmp")
    End If
    If KeyCode = vbKeyLeft Then
        Arrows.Left = Arrows.Left - 10
        Arrows.Picture = LoadPicture("LeftArrow.bmp")
    End If
    If KeyCode = vbKeyRight Then
        Arrows.Left = Arrows.Left + 10
        Arrows.Picture = LoadPicture("RightArrow.bmp")
    End If
End Sub
```

Mouse events

There are three mouse events that Visual Basic recognises, as shown in table 10.1:

Table 10.1 Mouse events.

Mouse Event	Description
MouseDown	A mouse button is pressed.
MouseUp	A pressed mouse button is released.
MouseMove	The mouse is moved from its current position.

The same MouseUp and MouseDown events occur irrespective of which mouse button is used. In order to find out which button is used, you must refer to an argument passed by Visual Basic to the event handler.

The MouseMove event

Whenever the mouse moves a MouseMove event occurs. The number of events which can be detected depends on the speed of your computer.

The header for the event procedure for a form is shown below:

> *Private Sub Form_MouseMove(Button **As Integer**, Shift **As Integer**, _*
> *X **As Single**, Y **As Single**)*

There are four parameters passed to the event procedure:

- The *Button* parameter indicates if any of the mouse buttons are pressed. If the left button is pressed the least significant bit of the parameter is pressed, the next least significant for the right button, and the next for the middle button. You can find which buttons have been pressed by applying the bit masks **vbLeftButton**, **vbRightButton** or **vbMiddleButton**. Any combination of these buttons can be set.
- The *Shift* parameter indicates the status of the **Shift**, **Ctrl** and **Alt** buttons. You can test to see which button is pressed by applying the bit masks **vbShiftMask**, **vbCtrlMask** and **vbAltMask**.
- *X* is the current x position.
- *Y* is the current y position.

If you want to track the movement of your mouse on a form only one line of code is needed in the Mouse Move event procedure:

> *Private Sub Form_MouseMove(Button **As Integer**, Shift **As Integer**, _*
> *X **As Single**, Y **As Single**)*
>
> > *Line -(X, Y)*
> *End Sub*

The **Line** method in the form shown draws a line between the previous position and the new position. which is passed to the event procedure. This produces the application shown running in figure 10.3.

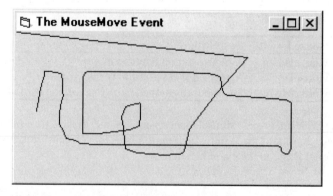

Figure 10.3 Tracking mouse movement using the MouseMove event.

The MouseDown and MouseUp events

When any mouse button is pressed and released, the MouseDown and MouseUp events occur. If you want to know what button was pressed you need to look at the *Button* parameter which is passed to the event procedure:

> **Private Sub** *Form_MouseDown(****Button As Integer****, Shift As Integer, _*
> *X As Single, Y As Single)*

The MouseUp event procedure has the same parameter list.

We can use the MouseDown event procedure to improve the previous application which tracked the movement of the mouse on the form. One of the problems with this application was that the starting position of the line was always the top left corner of the form, the 0,0 position. The second was that only one continuous line could be drawn. We are going to modify the application so that pressing any mouse button indicates the start of a line and pressing it again indicates the end of the line, so that you can draw many lines which are not connected. To do this we need to create a number of variables which will be available throughout the event procedures: that is they are defined in the General section:

> **Private** *XStart* **As Single,** *YStart* **As Single**   *' define in the General section*
> **Private** *Draw* **As Boolean,** *First* **As Boolean**   *'define in the General section*

The *XStart* and *YStart* variables are used to mark the start position of the line drawn in the MouseMove event procedure. The *Draw* boolean is **True** if a line is to be drawn when the MouseMove procedure is called and the *First* boolean is **True** when the MouseMove procedure is called for the first time after the mouse button has been pressed to indicate the start of a line. In the MouseMove procedure, a check is made to see if the *Draw* boolean is **True** and also to ensure that this is not the first point in the line. Only if *Draw* is **True** and *First* is **False**, is the line drawn. The state of the two booleans is set in the Form Load event which is executed when the application starts. The complete application is shown below:

> **Dim** *XStart* **As Single,** *YStart* **As Single**   *' define in the general section*
> **Dim** *Draw* **As Boolean,** *First* **As Boolean**
> **Private Sub** *Form_Load( )*
>   *Draw* = **False** *' toggles between drawing and non-drawing*
>   *First* = **True**   *' indicates if the current point is the start of the line.*
> **End Sub**
> **Private Sub** *Form_MouseDown(****Button As Integer****, Shift As Integer, _*
> *X As Single, Y As Single)*
> *' save the start position of the line*
>   *XStart = X*
>   *YStart = Y*
> *' we are changing between the draw and non draw mode*
>   *Draw* = **Not** *Draw*
> *' if we have just changed to drawing mode then the current position*
> *' is the start of the first line*
>   **If** *Draw* = **True Then** *First* = **True**

```
        End Sub
        Private Sub Form_MouseMove(Button As Integer, Shift As Integer, _
                                   X As Single, Y As Single)
        ' only draw a line if in drawing mode and this is not the first point
        If Draw And Not First Then Line (XStart, YStart)-(X, Y)
        ' save the current point as the start point of the line
            XStart = X
            YStart = Y
        ' the next time we come to this event procedure the new point cannot be the start
            First = False
        End Sub
```

The running application is shown in figure10.4.

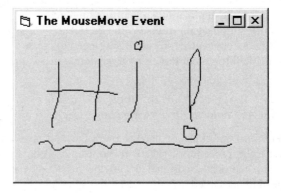

Figure 10.4 *The improved mouse tracking application.*

Dragging and dropping

Dragging and dropping are the techniques used to move a control from one position to another using the mouse. A control is selected by pressing a mouse button over the control to select it and then moving the mouse with the button still pressed. When the button is released the control is dropped into its new position.

Writing an application which uses drag and drop is not difficult, but it does require careful synchronisation between the **Drag** method and the two events, DragOver and DragDrop.

The Drag method

If you want to drag a picture you should use the **Drag** method to both start and end the dragging. The drag starts in the MouseUp event and ends in the MouseDown event. The general form of the **Drag** method is:

    *ControlName.**Drag** action*

The optional *action* parameter specifies the type of drag action taken as shown in table 10.2.

Table 10.2 *The action parameter of the **Drag** method.*

Value	Action
vbCancel	Cancel dragging.
vbBeginDrag	Start dragging the control.
vbEndDrag	Drop the control.

The default value for the *action* parameter is **vbBeginDrag** (start dragging the control).

The **MouseDown** event for the control which is to be dragged and dropped must contain a statement which allows the control to be dragged. When the mouse button is released the control is dropped into its new location.

To try the **Drag** method create an application which contains a PictureBox control and display a graphic by setting the **Picture** property. I used a picture of some high–tech equipment and therefore called the PictureBox *Technology*. The MouseDown event procedure for this control is shown below:

> **Private Sub** *Technology_MouseDown(Button **As Integer**, Shift **As Integer**, _*
> *X **As Single**, Y **As Single**)*
> *' Starts dragging the control*
> *Technology.**Drag vbBeginDrag***
> **End Sub**

When the mouse button is released the **Drag** method must be used again, but this time with the **vbEndDrag** parameter:

> **Private Sub** *Technology_MouseUp(Button **As Integer**, Shift **As Integer**, _*
> *X **As Single**, Y **As Single**)*
> *' Drops the control*
> *Technology.**Drag vbEndDrag***
> **End Sub**

If you try the application at this stage you will see a grey rectangle which represents the control being moved with the mouse, but when you release the button nothing happens. The final stage to make this a working application is to prepare the form to receive the dropped control in the form's DragDrop event procedure:

> **Private Sub** *Form_DragDrop(Source **As Control**, X **As Single**, Y **As Single**)*
> *Source.**Move** X, Y*
> **End Sub.**

Dropping the control in the correct position

When the control is dropped it appears to jump to a slightly different position and if you look carefully when the mouse button is pressed the control appears to jump then as well. Wherever the mouse is positioned over the control it is going to drag, when the mouse button is pressed, the drag icon is displayed with its centre on the mouse position. If you press the mouse button exactly in the centre of the control it will not jump. When the mouse button is released, it jumps so that its top left corner is in the position of the mouse. This is inconvenient, but we can overcome it with a straightforward calculation.

Since the mouse is positioned at the centre of the drag icon when the control is being moved and at the top left corner of the control when it is dropped, we know that it jumps vertically by half the height of the control and horizontally by half the width of the control. If we take this amount from the position the control is dropped on to in the DragDrop event, the control will not jump when the mouse button is released. The modified event procedure is shown below:

```
Private Sub Form_DragDrop(Source As Control, X As Single, Y As Single)
    X = X - (Technology.Width / 2)
    Y = Y - (Technology.Height / 2)
    Source.Move X, Y
End Sub
```

The size of the *Technology* control is given by its **Width** and **Height** properties.

The DragIcon method

When you move the control it would be an improvement if the control itself appeared to move rather than just a grey box. You can control the icon which is displayed when the mouse is dragging using the **DragIcon** property. If you make this equal to the **Picture** property of the PictureBox control, the control itself will appear to move when the mouse is dragged:

```
Private Sub Form_Load( )
    Technology.DragIcon = Technology.Picture
End Sub
```

The DragOver event

The **DragIcon** property can be used in conjunction with the DragOver event to indicate that the control being dragged is in an area of the form that does not accept a drop. The usual way of doing this is to change the **DragIcon** property into an appropriate symbol such as a stop sign when it passes over the forbidden area (usually a control) and back to normal when it leaves.

There is no code to prevent you from trying to drop the picture on to another control, but if you do so, nothing happens if there is no code in that control's DragDrop event processing to receive it.

The form of a DragOver event procedure for a control called *Image1* is:

Private Sub *Image1_DragOver (Source* **As** *Control, X* **As** *Single, _*
Y **As** *Single, State* **As** *Integer)*

The parameters are familiar from the other event procedures we have looked at apart from the *State* parameter. This can be one of three values: 0 indicates that the control being dragged has entered the control; 1 indicates it has left the control; 2 indicates that it is over the control.

In the event procedure shown below an Image control with the default name *Image1* has been added to the application. When the control called *Technology* is dragged over *Image1* the *State* parameter is 0 and the **DragIcon** property is changed to a stop sign. When the dragged control moves out of *Image1*, the *State* parameter is 1 and the **DragIcon** is changed back to the **Picture** property of the *Technology* control.

Private Sub *Image1_DragOver(Source* **As** *Control, X* **As** *Single, _*
Y **As** *Single, State* **As** *Integer)*
If *State = 0* **Then** *Technology.***DragIcon** *=* **LoadPicture***("c:\icons\stop.ico")*
If *State = 1* **Then** *Technology.***DragIcon** *= Technology.***Picture**
End Sub

If you try this application you need to specify a graphics file which exists on your system in the **LoadPicture** method, since the file used here will not exist on your system.

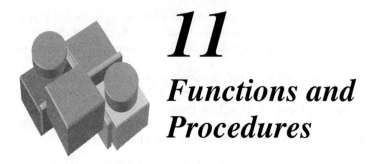

11
Functions and Procedures

Introduction

In a Windows environment whenever an event happens a block of Visual Basic statements called an event procedure is called. We have seen this in every application we have developed so far. In addition to using event procedures we can create our own procedures. A procedure is just a collection of Visual Basic statements, in the case of event procedures they are linked to visual components, while any other procedures we create are not. The advantage of creating new procedures rather than just writing all the Visual Basic code in event procedures is that a procedure may be called from more than one place, which reduces the need to duplicate code. Wherever possible it is best to reuse code as much as possible since it makes applications less complicated to test and reduces the number of possible errors. A function is very similar to a procedure except that it returns a value. In this chapter we are going to see how to create and use procedures.

The Password application

To see how procedures are used we are going to look at an application where a password is entered and checked to see if it is valid. If it is, a splash screen is displayed which in a full–scale application would provide a way into the application. If the password is incorrect a warning dialog is displayed. Up to three attempts are allowed after which the application unloads the form and ends.

When the application is run, the form shown in figure 11.1 is shown.

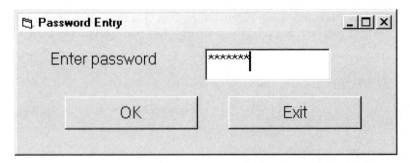

Figure 11.1 *The running password application.*

If an incorrect password is entered the message box on the left of figure 11.2 is shown. If the correct password is entered the message on the right of figure 11.2 is displayed.

Figure 11.2 *The application's message boxes.*

After entering the correct password and clicking on the **OK** button of the message box displayed, the splash screen shown in figure 11.3 is shown.

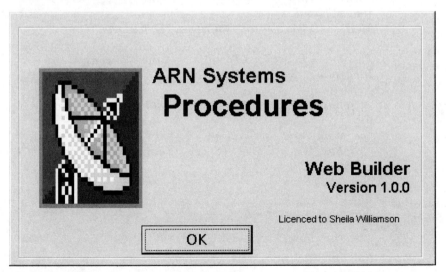

Figure 11.3 *The splash screen indicating that the correct password has been entered.*

If the correct password is not entered after three attempts, or if the **Exit** button is clicked, another message box (shown in figure 11.4) is displayed and the application ends.

Figure 11.4 The failed logon dialog.

To create this applications:

- On *Form1*, change the name of the TextBox to *Password* and the names of the buttons to *OK* and *Exit*.
- Change the **Password** property of the TextBox to *. This ensures that whatever character is typed on the * character will be displayed.
- Add a splash screen to the application using the **Project | Add Form** menu option and selecting the Splash Screen icon. You can edit the form created to create a splash screen with your own look.

The code for the two click event procedures for the two buttons is shown below:

```
Private Sub OK_Click( )
    Dim Password As String
    Static Attempts As Integer
' only allow 3 attempts before existing
    If Attempts = 2 Then
        Unload Form1
        MsgBox "Logon aborted", vbCritical, "Failed logon"
    Else
        Password = LCase(Pass.Text)          ' make lower case
        If Password <> "latinum" Then
' incorrect password
        MsgBox "Password not recognised", vbCritical, "Password check"
        Else
' correct password so enter the system
            MsgBox "Welcome to ARN Systems",vbInformation,"Password Check"
            Unload Form1
            frmSplash.Show
        End If
        Attempts = Attempts + 1
    End If
End Sub
Private Sub Exit_Click( )
' end the application
    MsgBox "Logon aborted", vbCritical, "Failed logon"
```

> **End**   *' ends the application*
> **End Sub**

Note that the integer variable *Attempts* is **Static** and therefore will retain its value after the event procedure has completed, and is not re–initialised every time it is run. The password is not case sensitive, therefore the **LCase** function is used to convert the text typed into lower case. The password which we are looking for is *latinum*.

The application functions well, but the event procedure for the *OK* button is rather too long and therefore difficult to debug, and it would be awkward to reuse the code elsewhere if there was a further logon process to use a restricted part of the system. We can break this application down into more manageable, reusable chunks by creating two new procedures.

Creating a procedure

To create a new procedure select the **Tools | Add Procedure** menu option. The dialog shown in figure 11.5 is displayed.

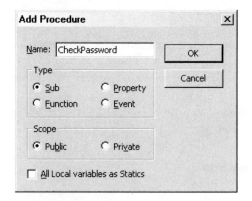

Figure 11.5 *Creating a new procedure.*

The procedure we are going to create is called *CheckPassword*. The procedure template shown below is produced.

> **Public Sub** *CheckPassword( )*
>
> ......
> **End Sub**

There are four types of procedures that you can create: the default type is **Sub**, which is the type we are going to use here; we are going to look at the **Function** type later. A procedure can be either **Public** or **Private** in scope. A **Public** procedure is accessible by all procedures in all modules in the application. A **Private** procedure is only accessible by other procedures in the module where it is declared.

The second procedure we are going to create is called *ExitApplication*.

These procedures can be called in two ways: you can either specify just the name of the procedure, or the name preceded by the word **Call**.

> *ExitApplication*

and

    Call *ExitApplication*

do exactly the same thing, but it is better to use the **Call** keyword to make it absolutely clear that you are calling a procedure which you have created yourself rather than using a standard Visual Basic procedure call.

The Click event procedure for the *OK* button can now be rewritten:

```
Private Sub OK_Click( )
    Static Attempts As Integer
' only allow 3 attempts before existing
    If Attempts = 2 Then Call ExitApplication Else Call CheckPassword
    Attempts = Attempts + 1
End Sub
```

The click event procedure for the *Exit* button can be rewritten:

```
Private Sub Exit_Click( )
' end the application
    Call ExitApplication
End Sub
```

Finally we have to write the code for our own procedures. The *ExitApplication* is called both in *OK_Click* and *Exit_Click*. It displays a message box and closes the applications:

```
Public Sub ExitApplication( )
    MsgBox "Logon aborted", vbCritical, "Failed logon"
    End                ' ends the application
End Sub
```

The *CheckPassword* procedure is shown below:

```
Public Sub CheckPassword( )
    Dim Password As String
    Password = LCase(Pass.Text)                ' make lower case
    If Password <> "latinum" Then
' incorrect password
        MsgBox "Password not recognised", vbCritical, "Password check"
    Else
' correct password so enter the system
        MsgBox "Welcome to ARN Systems", vbInformation, "Password Check"
        Unload Form1
        frmSplash.Show
    End If
End Sub
```

Functionally the application performs as before, but it has been broken down into more manageable pieces, which means that it can be debugged more easily and the procedures we have written can be reused within this application or another.

Passing parameters

Sometimes you may wish to pass information to a procedure, so that it can take different action depending on the data which is passed to it. In the next application shown running in figure 11.6, a grade between 0 and 100 is entered. The number of students and the average grade are calculated and displayed.

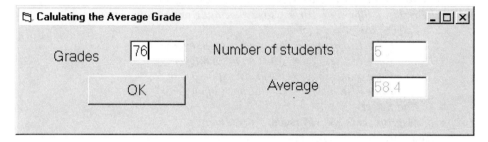

Figure 11.6 *Calculating average grades.*

Three error conditions are handled in this application:

- A grade greater than 100.
- A null grade.
- Entering any non–numeric value.

Depending on which of these errors occurs a different dialog is displayed. Figure 11.7 shows the dialog when a grade over 100 is entered.

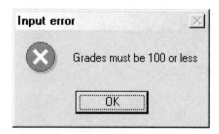

Figure 11.7 *The error dialog.*

When one of these errors is detected, a procedure is called and an integer is passed to it. Depending on the value of this integer a different error dialog is displayed. The advantage of using a procedure to handle the display of the error dialog is that you may want to display the same dialog from several different places in your application. If you want to make a change to the message you only have to do so in one place. If you do not perform your error handling centrally within a single procedure, it is easy make a mistake and to have slightly different text displayed when you want exactly the same message to be displayed. Users are quick to pick up on inconsistencies in applications, which gives a very unprofessional feel to the program.

To create this application:

- On *Form1*, change the name of the button to *OK* and the names of the TextBox controls to *Grade*, *Number* and *Average*.

- Set the **Enabled** property of the *Number* and *Average* TextBox controls to **False**, so that they can display information, but cannot take input from the keyboard.

The procedure called *ErrorMessage* takes a single integer parameter and depending on its value displays a different error message. The procedure is shown below:

```
Public Sub ErrorMessage(errorNumber As Integer)
' Display a different error message depending on the value passed
    Select Case errorNumber
        Case 1: message = "Must enter an integer value"
        Case 2: message = "Must input an integer"
        Case 3: message = "Grades must be 100 or less"
        Case Else: message = "unknown input error"
    End Select
    MsgBox message, vbCritical, "Input error"
End Sub
```

This procedure is called from three places in the application. In the KeyPress event procedure for the *Grade* TextBox a check is made to see if a non–numeric character has been entered:

```
Private Sub Grade_KeyPress(KeyAscii As Integer)
    If Not IsNumeric(Chr(KeyAscii)) And KeyAscii <> vbKeyBack Then
    Call ErrorMessage(1)
    End If
End Sub
```

The *ErrorMessage* procedure is called twice in the Click event handler for the *OK* button, when a grade of over 100 or a null value is entered:

```
Private Sub OK_Click( )
    Static NumberOfStudents As Integer
    Static Total As Integer
    If Grade.Text = "" Then
        Call ErrorMessage(2)
        Grade.Text = ""            ' clear the input TextBox
        ElseIf Grade.Text > 100 Then
        Call ErrorMessage(3)
        Grade.Text = ""            ' clear the input TextBox
    Else
        Total = Total + Grade.Text
        NumberOfStudents = NumberOfStudents + 1
        Number.Text = NumberOfStudents
        Average.Text = Total / NumberOfStudents
        Grade.Text = ""            ' clear the input TextBox
    End If
End Sub
```

Creating functions

A function is very similar to a procedure, the difference is that it returns a value. We have already seen some standard Visual Basic functions, for example the **Now** function returns the current date and time as a **Variant** data type.

> *Today = Now*

The **Now** function does not take any parameters, but both Visual Basic defined functions and your own functions can be passed parameters, for example:

> **Dim** *MyString* **As String**
> **Dim** *MyInt* **As Integer**
> *MyString = "1234"*
> *MyInt =* **CInt**(*MyString*)

The **CInt** function is a standard Visual Basic function which takes the string *MyString* as a parameter and returns an integer value. The integer *MyInt* is given the value returned by the function.

Since functions return a value they need to have a defined type; in the function shown below, the function *Biggest* takes three integer parameters. After the declaration of the parameters, the function type is specified, in this case **Integer**.

> **Public Function** *Biggest(a* **As Integer**, *b* **As Integer**, *c* **As Integer**) **As Integer**
>   *Biggest = a*
>   **If** *b > Biggest* **Then** *Biggest = b*
>   **If** *c > Biggest* **Then** *Biggest = c*
> **End Function**

The value returned is the value of the variable which has the function name, in this case *Biggest*.

This function can be called as follows:

> **Dim** *Result* **As Integer**
> *Result = Biggest(2333, 87, 878)*

The value returned is the largest number passed to the function, 2333.

Call by reference and call by value

There are two ways in which information can be passed to a procedure or a function, call by reference and call by value. The default used in Visual Basic is pass by reference.

When a parameter is passed to a procedure by reference the address of that data is passed, so that if you make any changes to that data item in the called procedure it will be changed in the calling procedure. This has some interesting repercussions on the scope of variables, since if you define a variable in a procedure it can only be changed in that procedure, unless you pass it by reference to another procedure where it can also be changed.

If you pass a variable by value a copy of that variable is made and passed to the called procedure. If you make any changes to that variable in the called procedure the original variable in the calling procedure is not changed.

Let us see how this works in practice by using a small procedure which uses pass by reference.

```
Public Sub Power(ByRef Value As Integer, ByRef Pow As Integer)
' raise Value to the power Pow and return the result in Value
    Dim c As Integer, Dim Result As Integer
    If Pow = 0 Then
        Value = 1              ' anything to the power zero is one
    ElseIf Pow > 1 Then
        Result = Value         ' anything to the power one is itself
        For c = 1 To Pow
        Result = Result * Value
        Next c
    Value = Result
    End If
End Sub
```

The keyword **ByRef** has been placed in front of the two variable declarations; it could have been omitted since pass by reference is the default, but it is good to make it explicit.

This procedure is passed two integer values called *Value* and *Pow*. *Value* is raised to the power *Pow* and the result returned in *Value*; if for example *Value* is 3 and *Pow* is 2, the procedure calculates 3^2 or 9. This could be called by the statement:

Call Power(a, b)

where both *a* and *b* are integer variables defined within the calling procedure which correspond with *Value* and *Pow* in the called procedure *Power*. Changing *Value* in *Power* results in the variable *a* changing even though *a* is defined as a local variable to the calling procedure. If the procedure *Power* was altered so that both parameters were passed by value, and the result printed in the Immediate window (using the **Debug.Print** statement) at the end of *Power* as shown:

```
Public Sub Power(ByVal Value As Integer, ByVal Pow As Integer)
' raise Value to the power Pow and return the result in value
    Dim c As Integer, Dim Result As Integer
    If Pow = 0 Then
        Value = 1              ' anything to the power zero is one
    ElseIf Pow > 1 Then
        Result = Value         ' anything to the power one is itself
        For c = 1 To Pow
        Result = Result * Value
        Next c
    Value = Result
    End If
```

> **Debug.Print** *Value*   *'prints the correct value in the Immediate window*
> **End Sub**

the correct result would be displayed in the Immediate window from *Power*. However, if you printed the variable *a* immediately after the call to *Power* in the calling procedure:

> **Call** *Power(a, b)*
> **Debug.Print** *a*   *'Value is unchanged - printed in the Immediate window*

the variable *a* would be unchanged, since only a copy of it had been passed to *Power*.

Note that to pass a variable by value (and to override the default of pass by reference), the parameter must be preceded by the **ByVal** keyword.

Where possible, call by reference should be avoided, since it alters the scope of variables and if you find that a variable has an unexpected value when debugging it makes it harder to find out where the problem occurred. It is often possible to design a procedure in a different way so that call by reference is not used. The *Power* procedure could easily be changed to become an integer function which returns the result and has two parameters passed to it by value. The only situation where it is not possible to use this approach is when you want to return more than one value from a procedure. In these circumstances perhaps it is better to write two functions rather than one procedure and to use pass by value.

Optional parameters

Visual Basic allows to pass optional parameters, that is parameters which may or may not be passed when the procedure is called. Optional parameters are listed in the procedure after the mandatory parameters and are preceded by the keyword **Optional**. We can add an optional *Error* parameter to the *Power* procedure:

> **Public Sub** *Power(**ByRef** Value **As Integer**, _
>   **ByRef** Pow **As Integer**, _
>   **Optional** Error **As Variant**)*
> **If IsMissing(***Error***) Then** *Error* = **False**
> ....

We can test to see if the parameter has been passed by the calling procedure by using the **IsMissing** function, which returns **True** if the parameter has not been passed. If **IsMissing** returns **True**, the usual action is to assign some default value to the missing parameter.

An alternative way of assigning a default value is to give the optional parameter a data type and to assign it a value within the parameter list, for example:

> **Public Sub** *Power(**ByRef** Value **As Integer**, _
>   **ByRef** Pow **As Integer**, _
>   **Optional** Error **As Boolean** = **False**)*

This is a more efficient implementation.

Using a start–up procedure

All of the applications we have seen so far have used a form as the start–up object. You can choose which form starts the application or specify a start–up procedure which must be called *Main*. To specify the start–up object choose the **Project I Properties** menu option to display the dialog shown in figure 11.8.

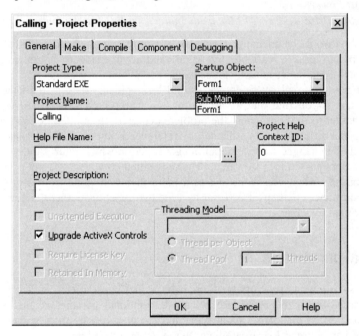

Figure 11.8 *Specifying the start–up object.*

The advantage of using a *Main* procedure to start an application is that the opening form of an application often contains a lot of controls and may take some time to load. If you use a main procedure you can display a splash screen welcoming the user and load the other forms into memory, so that when the user closes the opening splash screen the forms appear quickly. It does not actually make the application run any faster, it just avoids a wait at the start of the application while the initial form is loaded.

The main procedure should be placed in a separate code or BAS module. These modules are used to hold Visual Basic procedures and functions which are not related directly to the events which occur on a form. Code modules are also useful if you wish to create procedures or functions which are not closely linked to the event procedures of a particular form.

To create the BAS module select the **Project I Add Module** menu option to display the dialog shown in figure 11.9.

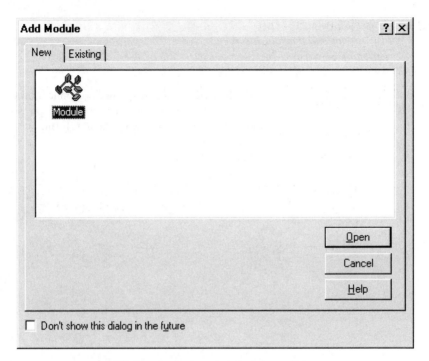

Figure 11.9 *Creating a code module.*

Click on the **Open** button to create the code module and add it to your project. The **Main** procedure can be added in the same way as any other module. The outline for the **Main** procedure is:

> ***Public Sub Main( )***
> ......
> ***End Sub***

The usual way it is used is to display a splash screen, using the **Show** method. The **Refresh** method ensures that the splash screen is fully displayed before further processing continues. Next, the remaining forms in the application can be loaded into memory, so that when the **Show** method is used the forms can be displayed very quickly. Any other lengthy background activities such as opening a database or establishing an internet link can be carried out at this point. Finally, the next form in the application is displayed and the splash screen unloaded to save memory. A typical main procedure is shown below:

> ***Public Sub Main( )***
>   *frmSplash.**Show***
>   *frmSplash.**Refresh***
> *' read form into memory but do not display*
>   ***Load** Form1*
> *' perform application initialisation*
> *' now display the form which is already loaded into memory*

```
    Form1.Show
' close and unload the splash screen
    Unload frmSplash
End Sub
```

It is a good idea to start a large applications like this, since an application which seems to have a very slow start–up can be very annoying for users, and it gives you a place to initialise the application which is not connected to a particular form.

12
Object–Oriented Programming

Introduction

Designing software which is efficient, meets requirements and is delivered on time is an extremely difficult activity. When hardware engineers design and build a new circuit, they use a set of existing components. They know how each of the components behaves and can express this mathematically, so they can predict with accuracy how the final piece of hardware they have designed will perform. A hardware engineer who refused to use any existing components and insisted on designing everything from the most basic elements would probably produce expensive, terrible designs and would quickly be out of a job. Until recently, however, when software engineers were designing a piece of software they would do exactly this. There are, for example, hundreds of word processor packages; they all do similar things and yet they have all been written from very low–level components. One of the key ideas of object–oriented programming is that reusable components can be used as the building blocks of our applications. We do this by creating classes.

Purists will rightly argue that Visual Basic is not an object–oriented language, however, it does allow you to use some aspects of object orientation. If you want to develop fully object–oriented applications you need to use a language such as Java.

In this chapter we are going to look at what classes and objects are and how to create and use them to create more robust applications.

Classes and objects

One of the key concepts in object–oriented programming (OOP) is the class. A class is a template or model which describes the data an object contains and the operations which can be performed on that data. A class is simply a description. If you want to use a class you must create an object, that is an instance of a class.

If you are not familiar with OOP these ideas may sound strange, but in fact we have already been using them. When we create a new control, for example a TextBox, we use the TextBox class which defines a set of properties and methods to create a TextBox object. You do this by selecting clicking on the control in the Toolbox and adding the control to a form. The Properties window lists the properties of the TextBox object we have created. If we create another TextBox we are creating another TextBox object. There is only one TextBox class, that is only one blueprint, but you can create as many objects belonging to this class as you wish.

Figure 12.1 shows the Properties window for an object called *Text1*, which is an instance of the TextBox class.

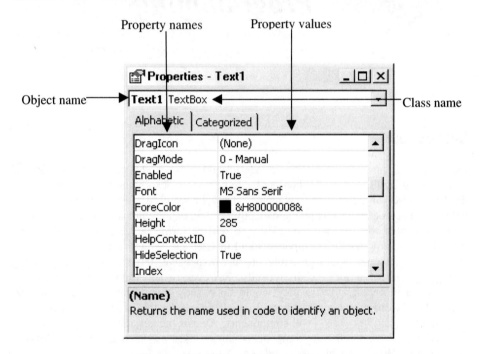

Figure 12.1 *Object classes and names.*

Classes define a list of properties which an instance of that class will have, for example the TextBox class states that an object belonging to it has a **ForeColor** property. Every TextBox object has a copy of this property with its own value. Changing the **ForeColor** property of one TextBox object does not change the **ForeColor** property of any other object.

Classes also define operations or methods which can be carried out on its objects, for example the **Show** method which displays a Form object.

The notation which we use to refer to the properties of an object is:

ObjectName.Property

for example:

*Text1.**Enabled** = **True***

The notation used to execute a method is the same:

ObjectName.MethodName

for example:

Form1.SetFocus

A method is a **Public** procedure or function in a class.

At this point you may be wondering what impact this is going to have on the way in which you can develop applications. There are two important new features which you can now begin to use:

- You can create and assign a variable to an object an run–time.
- You can create your own classes, which will have a defined set of properties or attributes and methods which perform operations on those properties.

Creating objects at run–time

You can create references to an existing object, that is you can assign an object (such as a control) to a variable. There are two stages to doing this:

- Declare an object variable as a member of a class, in a similar way to declaring a normal variable, using the **Dim** statement.
- Assign the variable to the object using the **Set** statement.

For example:

Dim *Text2* **As** *TextBox*

To assign values to the properties of the newly–created object you can use the **Set** statement. The syntax for this statement is:

Set *variable = object*

for example:

Set *Text2 = Text1*

Whenever you refer to the object *Text2*, it is the same as referring to *Text1*; for example, in an application with a single form containing a CommandButton with the default name of *Command1* and a single TextBox control called *Text1*, the event procedure for the Click event for the CommandButton is:

```
Private Sub Command1_Click( )
    Dim Text2 As TextBox
    Set Text2 = Text1
    Text1.Text = "hello"
    Text2.Top = Text1.Top + 100
End Sub
```

Since *Text1* and *Text2* refer to the same object, the single TextBox control has its **Text** property changed to *hello* and its **Top** property is increased by 100.

There are three possible reasons why you might wish to assign a variable to an object:

- The variable name be very long and awkward to use. If you assign the object to a variable you can use a more convenient variable name.
- You can change the variable to refer to another object while the application is running.
- Repeatedly referring to a variable rather than the object itself is more efficient.

User-defined classes

A more useful aspect is that you can create and use your own classes. A class module is used to define the class. To add a class module to your project choose the **Project | Add Class Module** option and click on the **Class Module** icon.

The class we are going to create is called *Employee*, which contains some data relating to individual employees and a method which is used for calculating an employee's salary. To create this application:

- Create a new class module from the **Project | Add Class Module** menu option, click on the **Class Module** icon.
- Change the name of the class module to *Employee*. This is the name of the class.
- To add data to this class define the following identifiers in the General section of the module:

> **Public** Name **As String**
> **Public** Hours **As Double**
> **Public** HourlyRate **As Double**
> **Public** Bonus **As Double**
> **Public** TargetMet **As Boolean**

These are called instance variables, since every instance of the *Employee* class, that is every *Employee* object, will have its own set of these variables which may have different values. This is the same as the way in which two TextBox objects have the same set of properties, but different values.

This class is going to have one method which defines how the salary for an employee is calculated. The salary is the number of hours worked multiplied by the hourly rate. If the productivity target has been met a bonus is added. The method called *Salary* is typed immediately after the declaration of the variables:

> **Public Function** Salary( ) **As Double**
>   Salary = Hours * HourlyRate
>   **If** TargetMet **Then** Salary = Salary + Bonus
> **End Function**

This has fully defined the *Employee* class, including all its data and its method. To create an instance of this class, that is an object in a module, we need to use a statement of the general form:

> **Dim** *ObjectName* **As New** *ClassName*

For example to create a new object called *Elizabeth* of type *Employee:*

> **Dim** *Elizabeth* **As New** *Employee*

To test this class and create an instance of it we are going to create an application as shown in figure 12.2.

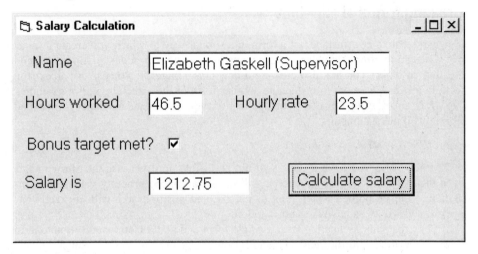

Figure 12.2 The user–defined Employee class.

The names of the top three TextBox controls have been changed to *EmployeeName*, *HoursWorked* and *HourlyRate*. When the application is run you need to enter values into these TextBox controls.

The name of the CheckBox control is changed to *BonusMet* and the final TextBox where the calculated salary is displayed is changed to *EmployeeSalary*.

The event procedure for the Click event of the CommandButton is shown below:

```
Private Sub Command1_Click( )
    Dim Elizabeth As New Employee
    Bonus = 120
    Elizabeth.Name = EmployeeName.Text
    Elizabeth.Hours = Val(HoursWorked.Text)
    Elizabeth.HourlyRate = Val(HourlyRate.Text)
    Elizabeth.Bonus = Bonus
    If BonusMet.Value = Checked Then
        Elizabeth.TargetMet = True
    Else: Elizabeth.TargetMet = False
    End If
    EmployeeSalary.Text = Str(Elizabeth.Salary)
End Sub
```

The **Dim** statement specifies that *Elizabeth* is an instance of the *Employee* class. The values typed for the employee name, hours worked, hourly rate and whether the productivity target has been met are copied to the instance variable of the *Elizabeth* object. When the *Salary* method of the *Employee* class is called, these values are used to calculate the salary which is returned by this function and is displayed. You can create as many objects of the *Employee* class as you wish; each will have its own set of instance variables.

Creating forms at run–time

You can create a new instance of a form in a similar way to which you create instances of classes you define yourself. When you create a new form at design–time, as well as creating an object you are also creating a new class: therefore you can use an existing form in a **Dim** statement to instantiate another form of the same class. For example, if *Form1* is an existing form in your application you can create a another form called *Form2* with the statement:

> **Dim** *Form2* **As New** *Form1*

The new form you have created will not be visible until you use the **Show** method; even then you will not see it, since it will inherit all of the property values of *Form1*, including the properties which control its size and position, so it will sit exactly on *Form1*, and will even have the same caption.

If you create an application with a single form and add a CommandButton to it, the Click event procedure for the CommandButton can be used to create a new form called *Form2* and to display it, by changing its position so that it is not exactly on top of *Form1* and using the **Show** method:

> **Private Sub** *Command1_Click( )*
> **Dim** *Form2* **As New** *Form1*
> *Form2.***Top** = *Form2.***Top** + *100*
> *Form2.***Left** = *Form2.***Left** + *100*
> *Form2.***Show**
> **End Sub**

This produces the running application shown in figure 12.3.

Since the second form, *Form2*, is of type *Form1*, it has the same property values as *Form1* and all of the controls placed on that form and their event procedures.

You can even use the **Dim** statement to create an array of forms in the same way in which you would create any other array, for example, to create an array of eleven forms of type *Form1*(which is an existing form):

> **Dim** *MyForm(10)* **As New** *Form1*

You can refer to the properties of one of these forms by statements of the general form:

> *ArrayName(IndexValue).Property = Value*

For example to increase the **Top** property of the first form in the array by 100:

> *MyForm(0).***Top** = *MyForm(0).***Top** + *100*

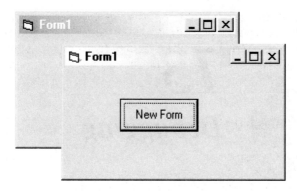

Figure 12.3 *Instantiating a new form.*

13

Debugging

Introduction

One of the most difficult aspects of writing software is that all software has bugs in it. Even if you write an application which is perfect, it is not possible to prove that it is completely without error. Visual Basic has some useful tools that help you to track down bugs in your application when it does not perform as expected. In this chapter we are going to look at different types of bugs and how to use the debugger to find out where problems are occurring.

What is debugging?

Not all of the applications that you write will work the first time! There are two main types of error:

- Syntax and semantic errors. These are caused when, for example, you mistype the name of a reserved word (**Nixt** instead of **Next**). This sort of error may occur when Visual Basic is unable to execute a line of your application because of some internal consistency, such as assigning a string identifier to an integer. These errors are fairly easy to find.
- Logic errors are much harder to correct. These are caused by some fault in your thinking when creating the application. Some logic errors may cause Visual Basic to report an error, while others will give an incorrect answer.

Visual Basic checks the syntax for individual lines of code at design–time and performs additional semantic checks at run–time. The line where the error has occurred is highlighted and a helpful message is displayed ~ this is usually enough to solve syntax problems. Logic errors or bugs are more complex: if a bug causes an application to crash completely at least you will know where it is crashing and there will be some message indicating what the problem is. If an application runs without crashing but produces the wrong answers it is usually much more difficult to find out where the problem began. The usual technique is to pause the execution of a running application and to examine the value of variables at that time to see if they are what you expect. If they are, you can execute a few more lines of the application and check the state of variables again, and so on until you can identify the region of the application where the problem starts.

The debugging process may sound simple, but it is one of the most difficult aspects of software development and although Visual Basic provides some excellent debugging tools, it still takes a lot of time and experience to become proficient at debugging applications.

The Debug tool bar

All of the debugging facilities can be found from the menu, but an easier way to access them is to use the Debug tool bar shown in figure 13.1.

Figure 13.1 *The Debug tool bar.*

If this tool bar is not displayed, right click in the tool bar area to display a speed menu which offers a list of tool bars which you can add to the IDE; choose the **Debug** option.

The icons are divided into three groups: running and pausing applications; using breakpoints; and displaying windows useful for debugging.

Running and pausing applications

The first group of icons is shown in table 13.1.

Table 13.1 *The Debug tool bar ~ run/stop section*

Icon	Equivalent menu option	Description
▶	**Run | Start**	Starts the application running from the beginning.
II	**Run | Break**	Breaks the running application.
■	**Run | Stop**	Stops the running application.

When an application is running you can pause it to enter a break mode by clicking on the break icon.

Breakpoints

If you want to examine the value of variables at specified points when the application is running, you need to break the application at a particular line. You can do this in a variety of ways:

- Place a **Stop** statement in the application.
- Press **Ctrl+Break** to break a running application.
- Insert a breakpoint.
- Step through the application, that is execute it a line at a time. Stepping automatically pauses after each line.

To insert and remove a breakpoint, position the cursor on the line where you want the program to pause and choose one of these options:

- Select the **Debug | Toggle Breakpoint** menu option.
- Choose the appropriate icon from the Debug tool bar as shown in table 13.2.
- Click on the vertical bar on the far left of the line.

The simplest option to use is the final one listed.

Table 13.2 *The Debug tool bar ~ toggling breakpoints.*

Icon	Equivalent menu option	Description
⍓	**Debug	Toggle Breakpoint**	Inserts or removes a breakpoint at the current cursor position.

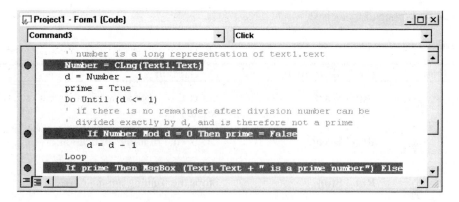

Figure 13.2 *Toggling breakpoints.*

The breakpoint is shown as a filled circle adjacent to the line as illustrated in figure 13.2.

Breakpoints are removed in the same way. You can have many breakpoints in your application, but more than ten makes it difficult to follow what is happening, and it is best to limit the number to one or two.

Stepping through an application

An alternative way of stopping an application is to use the step facility, which allows you to execute an application one line at a time, pausing after every line. You can start executing in this way from the start of the application by selecting the **Debug | Step Into** menu option, pressing **F8** or clicking on the corresponding icon as shown in table 13.3.

When an application is in break mode you can choose to step forward or to continue running the application so that it will execute until the next breakpoint is reached.

There are three forms of the step facility; you can choose which one you want from the menu or the icon on the Debug tool bar as shown in table 13.3.

Table 13.3 *The Debug tool bar ~ the step facility.*

Icon	Equivalent menu option	Description
	**Debug	Step Into**	Executes the next statement. If a procedure is called, the stepping continues through that called procedure.
	**Debug	Step Over**	Executes the next statement, but does not step into a procedure call.
	**Debug	Step Out**	Continues running the application, stopping at the line after which the current procedure was called.

- The **Step Into** option executes a single line of code and then breaks. If the statement it executes is a call to another procedure or function it steps into that procedure and will allow you to execute it a line at a time.
- The **Step Over** option will not step into a called procedure, but will treat the call to that procedure as a single line of code.
- The **Step Out** option allows you to jump to the line of the calling procedure at the line after the procedure was called.

You can switch freely between these modes.

The Run to Cursor command

If you only wish to break at a single point there is a simple command which allows you to do this. Position the curs or on the line on which you want to break and select the **Debug I Run to Cursor** menu option or press **Ctrl+F8**. When the application breaks you can position the cursor elsewhere and issue another **Run to Cursor** command.

Continuing and stopping

You can continue from a breakpoint in a variety of ways, by:

- Pressing **F5**.
- Selecting the **Run I Continue** menu option.
- Pressing the **Run** icon on the tool bar.

If you want to restart the application from the beginning you can choose from:

- Pressing **Shift+F5**.
- Selecting the **Run I Restart** menu option.

Displaying the value of variables

Using breakpoints you can stop an application at any point in its execution, but for this to be useful you need to be able to display the value of variables at this point to see if the values are what you expected. Visual Basic offers a variety of ways of doing this, including:

- Positioning the cursor on the variable.
- The Quick Watch Window.
- The Locals Window.
- The Immediate Window.

The first method is the simplest. If you click on a variable its value is displayed in the tool tip area as shown in figure 13.3.

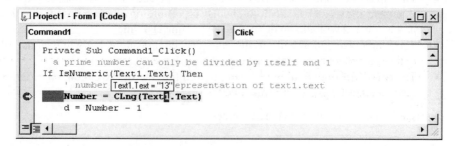

Figure 13.3 Displaying variable values.

The Quick Watch window

The Quick Watch window provides a quick way to find out the value of a variable. Click on the variable and select the **Debug | Quick** Watch menu option, click **Shift+F9** or click on the icon shown in table 13.4.

Table 13.4 *The Debug tool bar ~ displaying the Quick Watch window.*

Icon	Equivalent menu option	Description
	**Debug	Quick Watch**	Displays details of the current watch.

This causes the Quick Watch window as shown in figure 13.4 to be displayed.

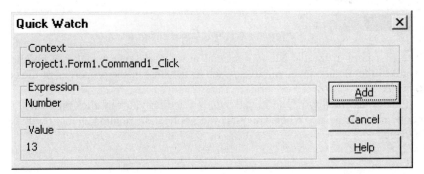

Figure 13.4 *The Quick Watch window.*

The value of the variable *Number* is 13.

The Locals window

The Locals window can be displayed by choosing the **View | Locals Window** or choosing the corresponding icon from the Debug tool bar as shown in table 13.5.

Table 13.5 *The Debug tool bar ~ displaying the Locals window.*

Icon	Equivalent menu option	Description
	**View	Locals Window**	Displays the Locals window.

The Locals window displays the value of all the variables in the current procedure. You can switch to see the variables in the calling procedure, or the procedure that called that procedure, and so on. The Locals window is shown in figure 13.5.

Click to change to a different procedure

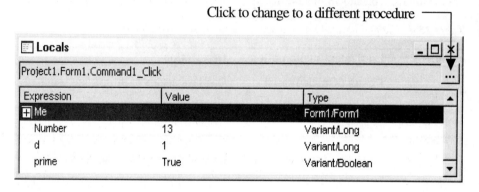

Figure 13.5 The Locals window.

The first item in the list **Me** is a special module variable, which can be clicked to show all of the module level variables, such as the state of the properties of the controls in this module.

An additional facility of the Locals window is that you can click on a value in this window and change it. When you start the application running again, it will use the new value.

The Immediate window

An alternative way of displaying values is to use the Immediate window, using the icon or menu command as shown in table 13.6.

Table 13.6 The Debug tool bar ~ displaying the Immediate window.

Icon	Equivalent menu option	Description
🖵	**View I Immediate Window**	Displays the Immediate window.

When you are at a breakpoint, if you click on the Immediate window to give it the focus you can display the value of any variables in scope by using ?, for example:

> *? Result*

displays the current value of the variable *Result*.

You can also print directly to the Immediate window from your application without breaking by using the **Debug.Print** method, for example:

Debug.Print *"The result is "* & Result

In addition to displaying the value of a variable in the Immediate window you can execute any valid Visual Basic statement.

Watch expressions

Sometimes when you are debugging an application you may wish to examine the value of some variables when a loop has executed many times. You could place a breakpoint within the loop and continue until it has looped the required number of times, but this is very boring and can take a long time. Another difficult situation which might arise is that you want to be informed when the value of a variable changes: you could do this by setting many breakpoints, but again it is difficult to do so. In these situations you can use watch expressions. When a watch expression you have set is met (perhaps a loop counter reaches a specified value) the application breaks.

To add a watch expression you need to use the Add Watch window, which can be displayed by selecting the **Debug | Add Watch** menu option or right clicking while in the code window and selecting the **Add Watch** option from the speed menu. The Edit Watch window, shown in figure 13.6, is displayed.

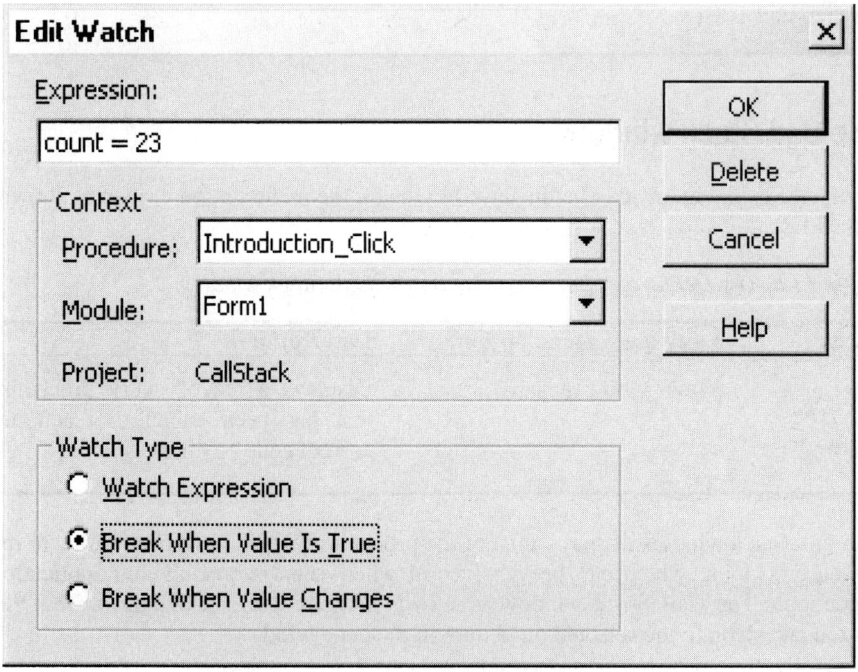

Figure 13.6 The Edit Watch window.

The **Expression** can be the name of a variable or any valid Visual Basic expression.

The **Context** specifies the variable's scope; you can restrict this to a single procedure in a single module or all procedures in all modules.

The **Watch Type** can be one of three options:

- **Watch Expression**. When this option is chosen the expression is evaluated and displayed whenever the application breaks.
- **Break When Value Is True**. When the expression is **True** the application breaks.
- **Break When Value Changes**. When the specified value changes the application breaks.

In figure 13.6, the application pauses when the variable *count* is 23.

If you wish to change a watch expression you can do so by selecting the **Debug | Edit Watch** menu option.

When the application breaks, the results of the watch are displayed in the Watch window, which can be displayed using the icon or menu command shown in table 13.7.

Table 13.7 *The Debug tool bar ~ displaying the Watch window.*

Icon	Equivalent menu option	Description
	**View	Watch Window**	Displays the Watch window.

The Call Stack window

The Call Stack window can be displayed by using the menu option or icon as shown in table 13.8.

Table 13.8 *The Debug tool bar ~ displaying the Call Stack window.*

Icon	Equivalent menu option	Description
	**View	Call Stack**	Displays a list of every procedure that has been called to reach the current code position.

The Call Stack window displays a list of the procedures which have been called to reach the current point, which can be very useful when you are tracing your application's execution. The Call Stack window is shown in figure 13.7. Clicking on the **Show** Button takes you to the selected procedure in the code window.

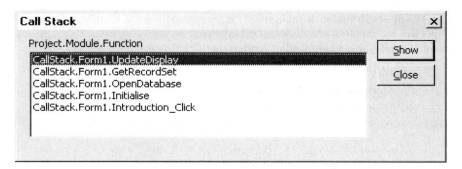

Figure 13.7 The Call Stack window.

Conditional compilation

Conditional compilation allows you to compile certain parts of an application depending on the value of a conditional compilation argument. This is useful, since when debugging you may put statements in your code which print debugging information. When the application seems to be working correctly you could take these statements out, but if a problem is found later you may have to put many of these diagnostic statements back. Visual Basic offers an easy way around this. You can specify one or more conditional compilation arguments, for example *DebugMode*, which you assign to -1 (**True),** if you wish the debug statements to be compiled. If this argument is **False**, the code specified is not compiled and is therefore excluded from the application, as if you had deleted it. If a problem arises you can simply change this argument to **True**.

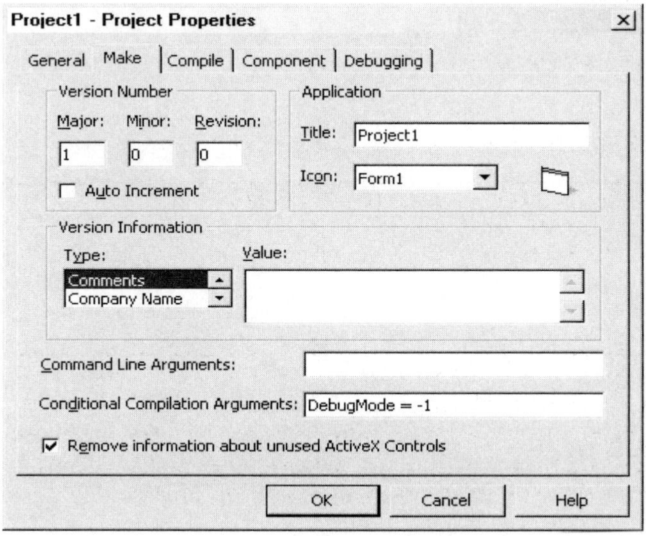

Figure 13.8 Specifying conditional compilation arguments.

To define the conditional compilation argument, select the **Project** | *ProjectName* **Properties** menu option and display the **Make** page as shown in figure 13.8.

In the **Conditional Compilation Arguments** TextBox insert the text:

DebugMode = -1

which sets it to **True**.

The conditionally–compiled code is enclosed within a **#** **If**...**Then**...**#EndIf** code block, for example:

> **#if** *DebugMode* **Then**   *' if DebugMode = -1 compile the following lines*
>   *' Debugging code goes here*
>   ......
> **#Else**   *' if DebugMode is not =-1 compile the following lines*
>   *' Alternative non-debugging code goes here*
>   ......
> **#End if**

If *DebugMode* is **True**, the code following the **#If**..**Then** statement is compiled, if it is **False** the code following the **Else** clause is compiled.

You can define multiple constants by separating them with a colon, for example:

DebugMode = -1:Diagnostic=0

An alternative way of achieving conditional compilation is to define a boolean with a **#Const** statement in the module in which you want conditional compilation to occur.

14

The Visual Data Manager

Introduction

Most real–world applications use a database to store and retrieve information. Visual Basic has one of the best development environments for creating database applications. Visual Basic even allows you to create databases and tables and to add information to them using the Visual Data Manager.

In this chapter we are going to see how to use the Visual Data Manager to create a database which we will use in applications in later chapters. If you use a database development environment such as Access you may prefer to use that rather than the Visual Data Manager to design your database and add information to its tables..

The flight booking system

In a relational database all information is stored in tables. Every row in a table contains information which relates to one entry in the table, for example if a table contained information on people working in a company each row would contain information on one person. Typical information would include the person's name, address, department, phone number, e–mail and so on. A column contains the same type of information about different people, for example a column might contain all of the names of people in the table.

The application we are going to develop with the Visual Data Manager is a flight booking system which has two tables, one containing the names, addresses and flight numbers of passengers and the other details of the flight. The *Passenger* table and some test data is shown in table 14.1

Table 14.1 *The Passenger table*

FirstName	SecondName	Address	PassengerNo	FlightNo
Tom	Wood	37 Ilkley Rd, Otley OT5 YK3. UK	TW003	BA5675
Sally	Wood	37 Ilkley Rd, Otley OT5 YK3. UK	SW004	BA5675
Vincent	Wilson	13 The Wharf, Newlyn, CN6 7TY. UK	VW125	BA6577
Borrelli	Gennarro	223 103rd St, LA, California 4365	BR873	VG9765
Charlotte	Lemay	67 Rue de Rivoli, Paris 3465, France	CL015	VG7639
Tony	Hudson	34 Matley St., Swindon, SN6 5RE. UK	TH652	VG7639

It is possible to have more than one person with the same name, you can usually distinguish between them by reference to the address, but even this is not guaranteed to work, since parents often name children after themselves or a grandparent. To avoid confusion each person who books a flight is assigned a unique passenger number.

Since there will be many passengers on one flight it is better to put all of the information relating to the flights into a separate table to avoid duplication of this information. The two tables are connected by sharing the *FlightNo* field which contains a unique value which identifies the flight. The *Flight* table is shown in table 14.2.

Table 14.2 *The Flight table*

Origin	Destination	DepartTime	ArriveTime	FlightNo
London	Venice	12:15	15:25	BA5675
London	New York	13:45	19:30	BA6577
Los Angeles	London	5:30	13:45	VG9765
Paris	London	12:30	13:30	VG7639

We are going to create these tables with the Visual Data Manager, add the data to them and create an application which can read the tables using SQL.

Creating a new database

The Visual Data Manager is an application which was written in Visual Basic 5.0. The source code is supplied by Microsoft with the Professional and Enterprise versions of Visual Basic.

To run the Visual Data Manager select the **Add–Ins I Visual Data Manager** menu option. The VisData window is displayed. The tables we are going to create must be within a database, therefore the first stage is to create the database itself.

The Visual Data Manager supports most of the most popular databases:

- Microsoft Access versions 2.0 and 7.0.
- Dbase versions III, IV, 5.0.
- FoxPro versions 2.0, 2.5, 2.6 and 3.0.
- Paradox versions 3.x, 4.x, and 5.0
- ODBC. Open Database Connectivity is an Applications Programming Interface (API) which defines how an application can access data in a data source using a defined set of API functions, Data Access Objects (DAO) or Remote Data Objects (RDO). ODBC databases include SQL Server and Oracle.
- Text files in formats such as Excel and Lotus 1–2–3 can also be referenced as if they were databases.

The database we are going to select is Access version 7.0. To create this database select the **File** | **New** | **Microsoft Access** | **Version 7.0 MDB** from the VisData menu as shown in figure 14.1.

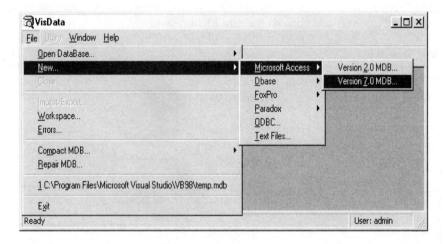

Figure 14.1 *Creating a new Access version 7.0 database.*

You can browse your file system, to choose the location and name of your database. Specify the name of the database as *FlightBookingDatabase*. After creating the database we have to create the tables and add the data to them.

Creating the Passenger table

To create the *Passenger* table, right click on **Properties** in the Database Window as shown in figure 14.2. Click on the **New Table** option to create an empty table.

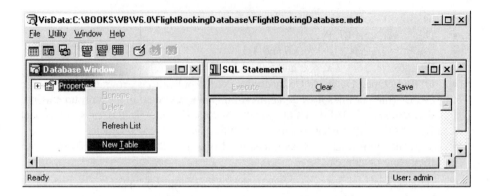

Figure 14.2 *Creating the Passenger table.*

The Table Structure window is displayed as shown in figure 14.3. Enter the name of the table as *Passenger* and click on the **Add Field** button.

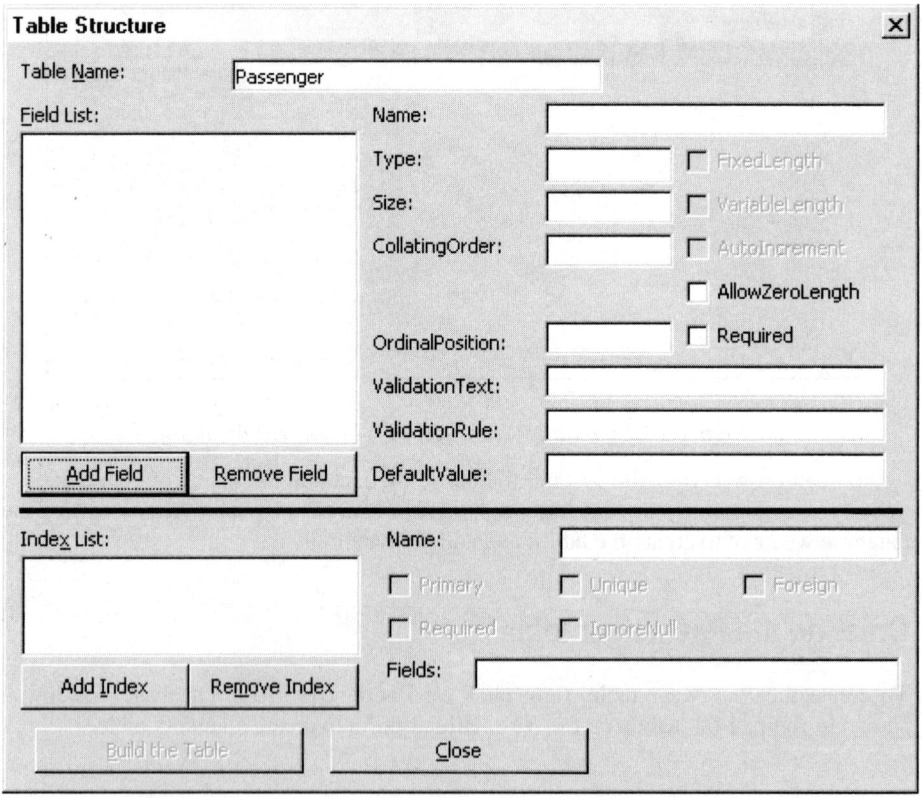

Table Structure

Table Name: Passenger

Field List:

Name:

Type: ☐ FixedLength

Size: ☐ VariableLength

CollatingOrder: ☐ AutoIncrement

☐ AllowZeroLength

OrdinalPosition: ☐ Required

ValidationText:

ValidationRule:

[Add Field] [Remove Field] DefaultValue:

Index List:

Name:

☐ Primary   ☐ Unique   ☐ Foreign

☐ Required   ☐ IgnoreNull

[Add Index] [Remove Index] Fields:

[Build the Table] [Close]

Figure 14.3 *Adding fields to the Passenger table.*

The fields correspond to the name columns in the *Passenger* table. There are five fields in this table:

- *FirstName* ~ text 10 characters long.
- *SecondName* ~ text 15 characters long.
- *Address* ~ text 50 characters long.
- *PassengerNo* ~ text 5 characters long
- *FlightNo* ~ text 6 characters long.

Clicking on the **Add Field** button displays the Add Field dialog. The first field we are going to add is *FirstName*. This is of type **Text** and is 10 bytes long as shown in figure 14.4.

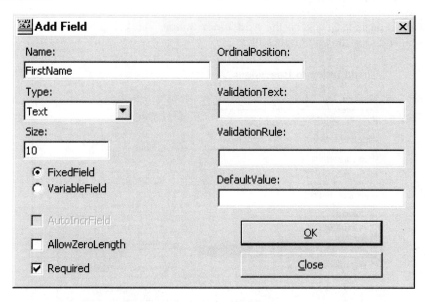

Figure 14.4 Specifying field details.

This field is of fixed size and cannot be changed by users. It is mandatory and it cannot be a zero–length string.

The **OrdinalPosition** specifies the position of the field relative to other fields in the table. If you do not enter a value, Visual Basic will order the fields in an unspecified way.

The **ValidationRule** allows you to specify a rule which the data entered must meet, for example a range of values could be specified for an integer field.

The **ValidationText** is the message displayed if an invalid value is entered, that is one which does not meet the **ValidationRule**.

It is not mandatory to enter the **OrdinalPosition**, **ValidationRule** or **ValidationText** fields.

Click on the **OK** button to add the *SecondName*, *Address PassengerNo* and *FlightNo* fields. They are all mandatory, fixed size and do not allow zero–length strings to be entered.

Click on the **Close** button to return to the Table Structure dialog.

If there is a field upon which most of the database searches will be based, such as a surname, you can speed up the searches by creating an index. The database engine

maintains and updates the index for you. Although searches are speeded up, updates to
the table are slowed down, since the index also needs to be updated. The index also
takes up disk space which may be considerable. Despite these problems, indexes
provide such an increase in speed, particularly for large databases, that they are very
worthwhile. In this example the index is based on the field *PassengerNo*. This is main
or primary key and each entry is unique since no two passengers share the same
passenger number. In this database if one person books two different flights he will
have different passenger numbers for each flight. If we wanted to have the same
PassengerNo for different flights the index would not be unique. Ideally an index
should be unique.

To add an index click on the **Add Index** button. This displays the Add Index to
Passenger dialog shown in figure 14.5.

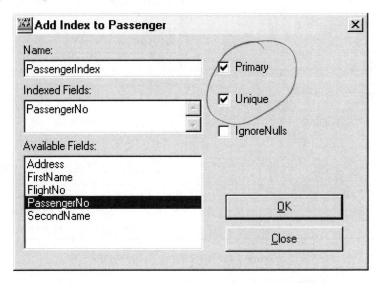

Figure 14.5 *Adding an index to the Passenger table.*

You can choose more than one field to be a part of the index, but usually only one
field is chosen, in this case *PassengerNo* is used. Specify that it is **Primary** and
Unique. It is given the name *PassengerIndex*. Click on the **OK** button to return to the
Table Structure dialog, which should appear similar to figure 14.6. At this stage you
can change some of the attributes of a field but not the type of data it represents or its
size. If you wish to change these, delete the field which is incorrect and enter it again.
To create and build the table click on the **Build Table** button.

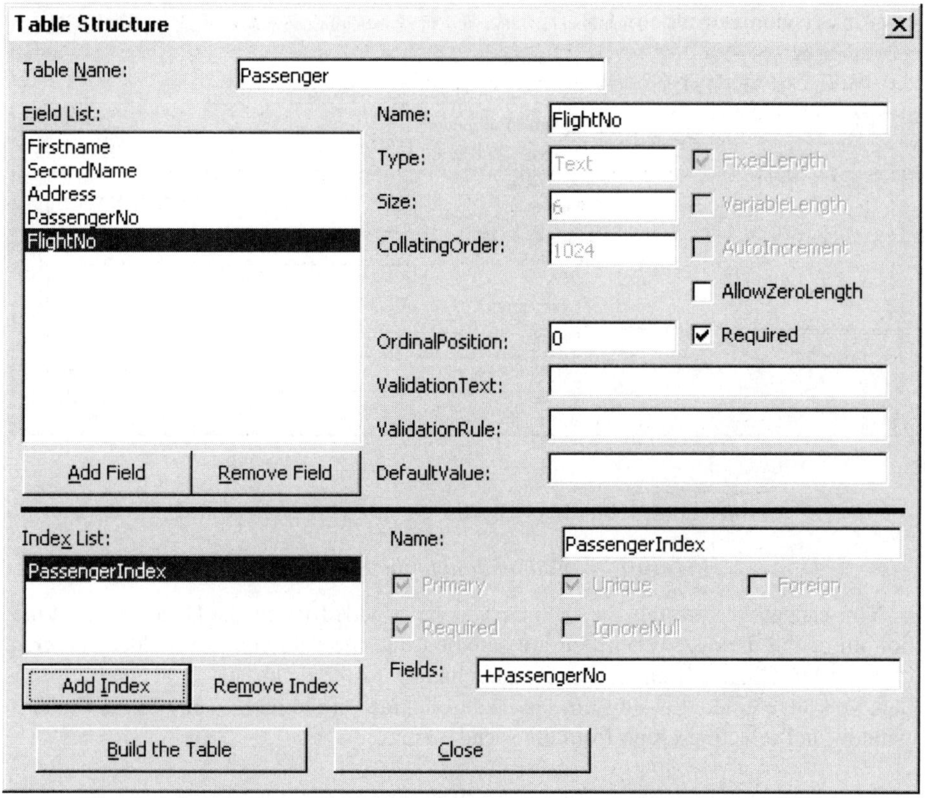

Figure 14.6 *Building the Passenger table.*

This creates the table structure, but there is still no data within it.

Add data to the Passenger table

To add data to the passenger table, right click on the table name in the Database Window to show the speed menu and select the **Open** option. If you wish to return to the Table Structure dialog select the **Design** option from the speed menu.

Each row in the table can now be entered. After entering one row click on the **Update** button to save the data. To add another row click on the **Add** button (which replaces the **Cancel** button shown in figure 14.7 after the **Update** button has been pressed).

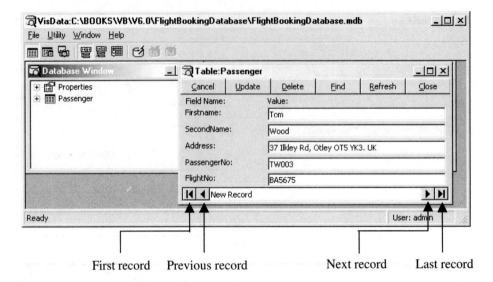

First record   Previous record   Next record   Last record

Figure 14.7 *Adding data to the Passenger table.*

You can move through the records you have added using the Data control at the bottom of the dialog. When you are satisfied that the data you have added is correct click on the **Close** button to commit the changes to the database. You can revisit the data you have entered at any time by right clicking on the table name in the Database window and selecting **Open** from the speed menu.

Creating the Flight table

The *Flight* table is created in a similar way to the *Passenger* table. Right click on **Properties** in the Database window and select the **New Table** menu option. Specify that the new table's name is *Flight*. It contains five fields:

- *Origin* ~ text 15 characters long.
- *Destination* ~ text 15 characters long.
- *DepartTime* ~ date/time.
- *ArriveTime* ~ date/time.
- *FlightNo* ~ text 6 characters long.

Add a primary index based on the unique *FlightNo* field which is called *FlightIndex*. The Table Structure dialog just before pressing the **Build the Table** button should be similar to figure 14.8.

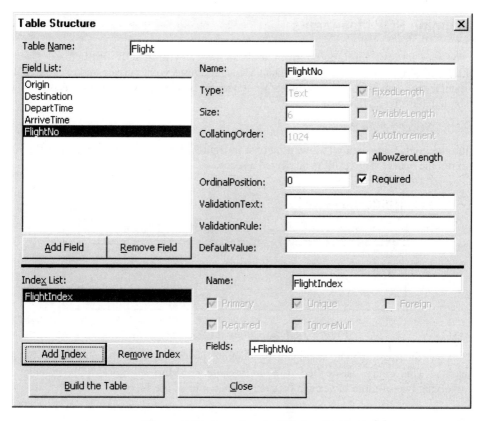

Figure 14.8 Creating the Flight table.

To add the data right click on the table name in the Database window and select the **Open** menu option.

One–to–many relationships

If every row in a table is related to exactly one row in another table there is a one–to–one relationship between the tables. This is an unusual situation, but an example is a database where information on an individual is stored in two separate tables: one table contains non–confidential information on the person, while a second table contains confidential information, such as medical records, perhaps for security reasons. There is always a one–to–one relationship between the rows in the two tables.

A more common relationship is where there is a one–to–many relationship. This exists between the *Flight* and *Passenger* tables. For each flight, that is for every row in the *Flight* table, there may be more than one passenger, that is many rows in the *Passenger* table. The two tables are connected by sharing a common flight number.

Running SQL statements

You can retrieve information from a database by writing SQL (Structured Query Language) statements. The Visual Data Manager allows you to create and execute SQL statements. The simplest possible SQL statement is to display all of the records in a single table. To do this type:

> *Select * from Passenger*

into the SQL Statement window, as shown in figure 14.9. Click on the **Execute** Button to run the query. The result is displayed a record at a time.

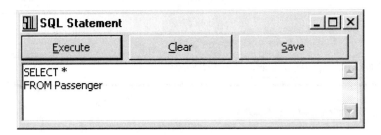

Figure 14.9 Executing an SQL statement.

You can save an SQL statement by clicking on the **Save** button and specifying a name. This query was called *AllFromPassenger*. More complex SQL statements involving two or more tables can be used as shown in figure 14.10.

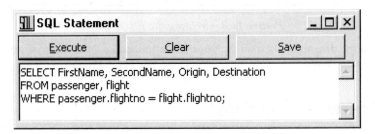

Figure 14.10 An SQL statement with two tables.

The effect of this SQL statement is to extract the *FirstName* and *SecondName* from the *Passenger* table and the *Origin* and *Destination* from the *Flight* table where the flight number is the same in both tables. For example, since Vincent Wilson's flight number is VG9765, the row in the *Flight* table for this flight number is found and the *Origin* and *Destination* extracted to shown that Vincent is flying from London to New York. This query was saved as *FirstSecondOriginDestination*. The results of executing this SQL statement are shown in figure 14.11.

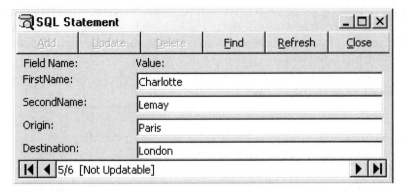

Figure 14.11 *The results of executing an SQL statement.*

You can move through the results of executing the SQL statement using the Data control at the bottom of the dialog.

The Database window shown in figure 14.12 contains not only the two tables in the database but also the two QueryDefs which we have created.

Figure 14.12 *The Database Window showing the QueryDefs.*

If you right click on a QueryDef the speed menu displayed offers you a variety of options for modifying or running the query.

Recordsets

When you carry out a query on a database, a collection of records is returned. If, for example, you execute an SQL enquiry such as:

Select *FirstName, SecondName* **from** *Passenger* **where** *FlightNo = VG7639* all of the passengers on flight *VG7639* will be returned. This collection of records is called the recordset. When you attempt to move beyond the end of the record you are at the EOF (end of file) and a phantom record is created after the last record in the record set as shown in figure 14.13.

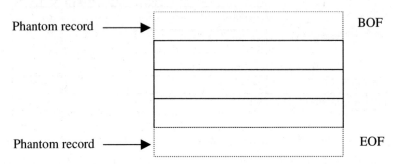

Figure 14.13 *The Recordset and phantom records.*

Similarly when you attempt to move before the start of the recordset a phantom record is created and you are at the BOF (beginning of file).

The Data Form Designer

Another useful utility in the Visual Data Manager is the Data Form Designer which you can run using the **Utility** I **Data Form Designer** menu option in the Visual Data Manager. The Data Form Designer is shown in figure 14.14.

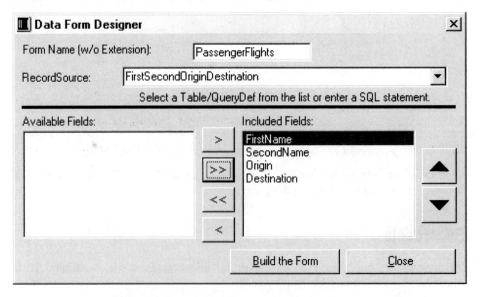

Figure 14.14 *Running the Data Form Designer.*

This utility builds a form which is added to the current application. The form will read records from the record source which may be either a single table or a query based on an SQL statement.

- Give the new form which the Data Form Designer will build the name *PassengerFlights*. This will create a form with the name *frmPassengerFlights*.
- The **RecordSource** may be a table, in which case all of the columns in that table are listed in the **Available Fields** list. You can specify a QueryDef, that is an SQL statement which you have saved earlier. In this case use the QueryDef which we called *FirstSecondOriginDestination*. The four fields returned by this query are displayed in the **Available Fields** list.
- To move fields from the **Available Fields** list to the **Included Fields** list use the keys with the horizontal arrows. The single arrow moves a selected item. The double arrow moves all items. The form created will only display the fields listed in the **Included Fields** list.
- You can change the order of the included fields by using the two keys with the vertical arrows. The selected field moves in the direction of the arrow pressed.
- To complete the form click the **Build the Form** button.
- The form is cleared and you are given the opportunity to build another form. Since we only want to create one form click on the **Close** button to leave the Data Form Designer.

To view the form we have created, close the Visual Data Manager to return to Visual Basic, where you will see the form created listed in the Project Explorer.

The form is shown in figure 14.15.

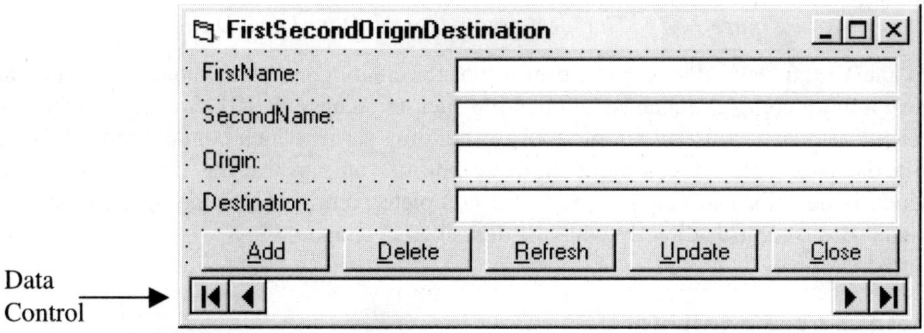

Figure 14.15 The form created by the Data Form Designer.

The control at the bottom of the form is a Data Control which provides a connection to the data source. Clicking on the inner arrows moves to the previous or the next **Recordset** object. The outer arrows move directly to the first or last object.

We look at the Data control and how it is used to build database applications, in detail, in the next two chapters.

Running the application

If you added the form created to a standard EXE project, you will have a form with the default name *Form1* as a part of your project. You can remove this form by closing it and then right clicking on *Form1* in the Project Explorer to reveal the speed menu. Click on the **Remove from Project** option.

To ensure that the form which we have created is executed first when the application runs choose the **Project | Properties** menu option and change the **Startup Object** to the name of the new start–up form, in this case *frmPassengerFlights*.

When the application is run as shown in figure 14.16 you can view the data retrieved, delete it, amend it, or add new data.

Figure 14.16 *The form created by the Data Form Designer.*

The Visual Data Manager is a useful tool for creating simple databases if you do not have a more complex database application such as Access or SQL Server, and the Data Form Designer is a useful simple tool for building forms which contain controls linked to a database. But if you want more flexibility you can use the Data Form Wizard which is described in chapter 15, or for complete control create the application using Visual Basic controls directly which is described in chapter 16.

Data–aware controls

The Data control provides a connection between the data source and the application. The data that it reads is specified in the **RecordSource** property of the Data control. This is in the form of an SQL statement. The Data Form Designer and the Data Form Wizard set up this property for you. The Data control is essential to provide the connection between the data source and the application, but how are the fields from that data source connected to the text fields, so that when we request a new record to be displayed the contents of the text fields are displayed? TextBox controls, along with most of the other standard controls and many of the ActiveX controls, are said to be data–aware: that is, you can connect the control to a data source and specify which field of that record source it is to display. The **DataSource** property of the control provides the connection to the data source and the **DataField** property specifies the field of that data source which is to be displayed. The Data Form Designer and also the Data Form Wizard set up these properties for you, but as we will see in chapter 16 it is straightforward to set them up for yourself when you are creating your own custom database applications.

15

The Data Form Wizard

Introduction

The Data Form Wizard is a flexible tool which creates forms which execute a single query. The queries can be related to a single table in a database or to a query which uses many tables. When a query is executed a **Recordset** object is produced that represents all of the records, returned by the query. The Data Form Wizard allows you to create forms which display the query results one record at a time, or many records using a grid. The Data Form Wizard uses the ADO (ActiveX Data Object) control rather than the Data control and therefore can access databases which are either local or remote.

Running the Data Form Wizard

You can run the Data Form Wizard by selecting the **Add–Ins I Data Form Wizard** menu option. If this option is not available, choose the **Add–Ins I Add–In Manager** menu option and select the **VB 6 Data Form Wizard** option as shown in figure 15.1. Click on the **Load/Unloaded** check box and the **Load on Startup** check box to ensure that it is available for this application and will subsequently be available from start–up for other applications.

When the Data Form Wizard is first run, you are asked for a profile. This is a record of the settings you have chosen when you have run the Data Form Wizard on previous occasions. You are prompted at the end of using the Data Form Wizard to specify if you wish to save the choices you have made as a profile. If you do, this profile will be available when you next run the Data Form Wizard. If you do not want to use a profile choose the **(None)** default.

Clicking on the **Next** button on the first form of the Data Form Wizard moves to the next form which allows you to specify the type of database you are using.

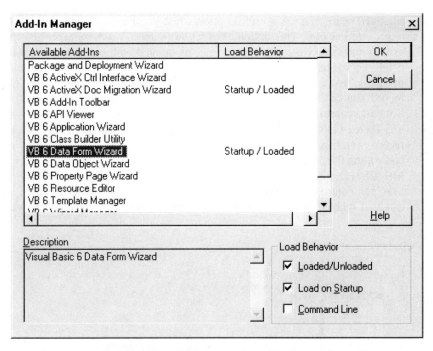

Figure 15.1 *Running the Add–In Manager.*

Choosing the database

You can choose from two types of databases, **Access** or **ODBC**. ODBC (Open Database Connectivity) is a standard protocol which consists of a set of routines which allows Windows applications to access a database across a network.

The database we are going to connect to is called *FlightBookingDatabase* which we created in the previous chapter. This is an Access database so you should choose the Access option.

Click in the **Next** button to proceed or the **Previous** button to return to the previous form.

The next form prompts you for the name of your database. You can browse through your file system for the Access database you want to use.

Choosing the format

The next form shown in figure 15.2 prompts for the name of the form which is created and the layout of the form. There are five options:

- **Single Record**. Displays the results of the query one record at a time.
- **Grid (Datasheet)**. Displays the query results in a DataGrid control.

- **Master/Detail**. This is a useful option when you have two tables in a one–to–many relationship. This option allows you to specify a master record source ~ usually the table which has many rows associated with each of its rows, and a detail record source. In this example we are going to use the *Flight* table as the master source and the *Passenger* table as the detail record source. The master record source is displayed a record at a time and the detailed source in a DataGrid control below it.
- **MS HFlex Grid.** Displays the records in a FlexGrid control. This displays the records returned by the query in a tabular format and has many options for controlling the appearance.
- **MS Chart.** This option can only be chosen to display the records in an MSChart control if the record source contains at least two numeric values, which can be displayed in a variety of graphical ways including bar and pie charts.

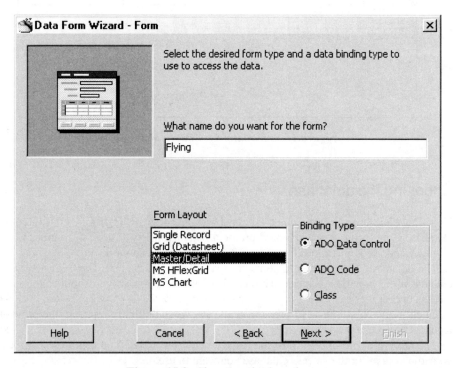

Figure 15.2 Choosing the form layout.

You can also specify how your form is to be connected to the data source. Choose the **ADO Data Control** option to include this control on your form for connecting the data source to your form. The **ADO Code** and **Class** options replace the ADO data control with a collection of labels and buttons which looks the same and functions in a similar manner. The difference in using these two options is that you can see and modify the code used to access the data source. The **ADO Code** option includes all of the code within the code module which handles the form's events. The **Class** option creates a class file which contains code to access the data.

For this application choose the **Master/Detail** option with the **ADO data Control** options. Click on **Next** to proceed.

Setting the master record source

This form, shown in figure 15.3, allows you to choose the master record source, in this case the table *Flight*, and lists all of the available fields.

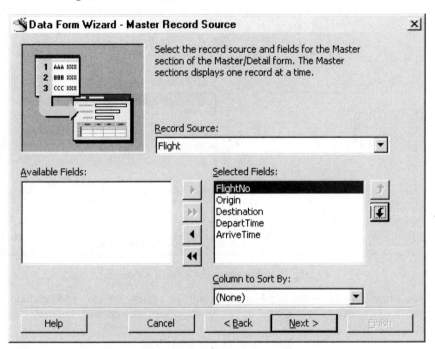

Figure 15.3 Specifying the master record set.

Clicking on the single horizontal arrows between the **Available Fields** and the **Selected Fields** moves the selected fields. Clicking on the double arrows moves all of the fields. The vertical arrows on the right of the **Selected Fields** moves the current selected field to a new position. This position determines where the fields will appear on the completed form. Use these keys to give the order shown in figure 15.3.

You can choose the order in which the results of a query are displayed by choosing a field (that is a column in a table) from the **Column to Sort By** list.

Setting the detail record source

For every single flight there are many passengers. The master record specified gives details of a flight and the detail record source gives all of the passengers booked on that flight. In this example the **Record Source** is the *Passenger* table and we wish to display all of the fields. Place the selected fields in the order shown in figure 15.4.

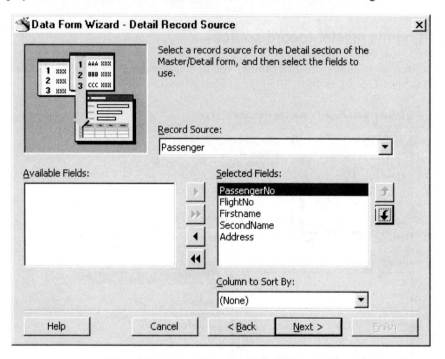

***Figure 15.4** Specifying the detail record set.*

You can choose the order in which the results of a query are displayed and move to the previous or next stage of the wizard as for the other forms in the sequence. Click on **Next** to proceed.

Connecting the data sources

The one–to–many relationship is achieved by the two tables, *Flight* and *Passenger* sharing a common field or column. In this case the column is *FlightNo*. It is usual to give common fields the same name , so that it is immediately clear that they contain the same information, but this is not mandatory. Clicking on the *FlightNo* field for both the **Master** and **Detail** field list, shown in figure 15.5, ensures that when a record is displayed for the master record source with a particular *FlightNo* value, the corresponding passenger details are displayed for passengers which have the same *FlightNo*.

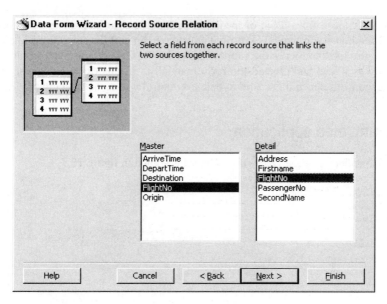

Figure 15.5 *Connecting the master and detail record set.*

Selecting the controls

This is the final stage of the wizard, shown in figure 15.6.

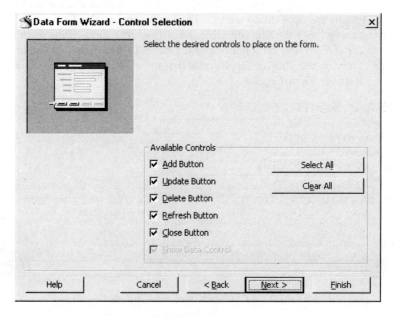

Figure 15.6 *Selecting the controls.*

You can choose from a list of available buttons what to include on your completed form. The choice you make is not final since you can edit the form and add additional controls (provided you write the supporting Visual Basic code) or delete controls, in the same way as if you had created the form manually. In this example choose all of the available controls, since it is easier to delete a control you do not want than to add one.

The completed application

The form produced by the Data Form Wizard is shown in figure 15.7.

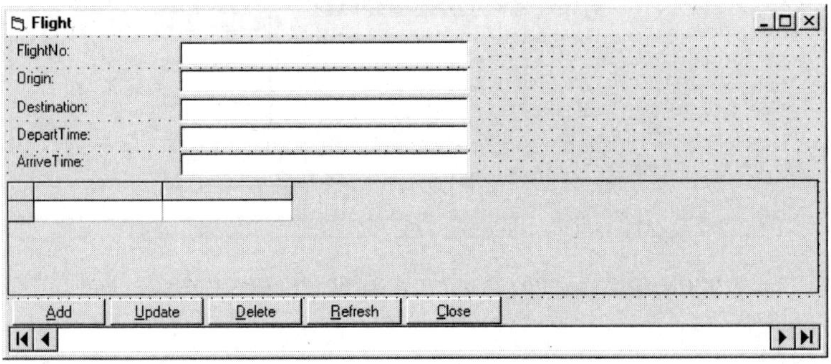

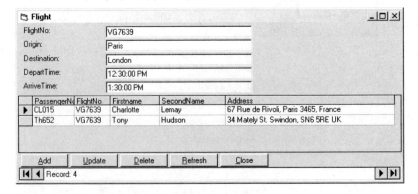

Figure 15.7 *The completed application at design–time.*

Before you can run the application you need to increase the size of the DataGrid which is used to display the passenger details. You also need to change the form which is executed when the application starts. To do this choose the **Project I Properties** menu option and change the **Startup Object** to *Flying*, the name of the form which the wizard has created. If you no longer need the default form *Form1* in the application, select that form in the Project Explorer and right click to reveal the speed menu. Choose the **Remove Form1** option.

Figure 15.8 *The completed application at run–time.*

The running application is shown in figure 15.8.

As you move through the Flight table using the Data control, the passengers with the same flight number are displayed.

How flexible is the Data Form Wizard?

The Data Form Wizard can create forms which presents data in a variety of ways, for example, figure 15.9 displays the *Flight* table in a DataGrid.

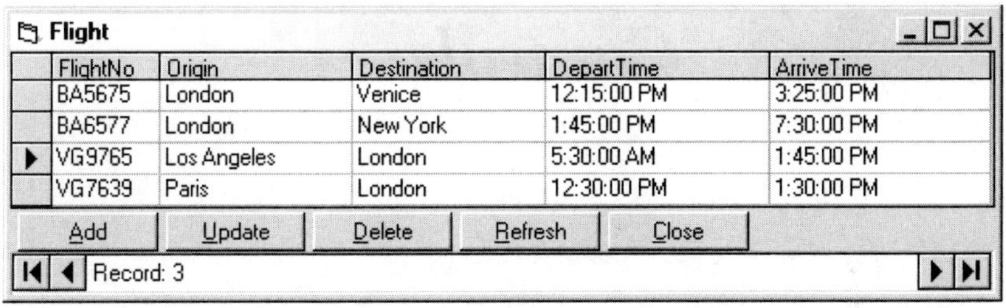

FlightNo	Origin	Destination	DepartTime	ArriveTime
BA5675	London	Venice	12:15:00 PM	3:25:00 PM
BA6577	London	New York	1:45:00 PM	7:30:00 PM
VG9765	Los Angeles	London	5:30:00 AM	1:45:00 PM
VG7639	Paris	London	12:30:00 PM	1:30:00 PM

Figure 15.9 *Flight details displayed in a DataGrid.*

Figure 15.10 displays the same table in one of the formats offered by the FlexGrid.

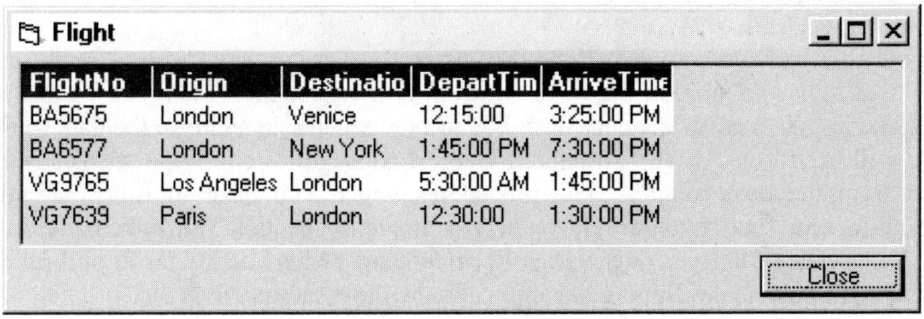

FlightNo	Origin	Destinatio	DepartTim	ArriveTime
BA5675	London	Venice	12:15:00	3:25:00 PM
BA6577	London	New York	1:45:00 PM	7:30:00 PM
VG9765	Los Angeles	London	5:30:00 AM	1:45:00 PM
VG7639	Paris	London	12:30:00	1:30:00 PM

Figure 15.10 *Flight details displayed in a FlexGrid.*

If you have numerical data, for example the number of free seats and the price of the seats, you can display this in a MSChart component.

For many straightforward database systems you can use the Visual Data Manager or the Data Form Wizard, but if you want total control over your database applications you need to write the application yourself using data–bound controls and SQL queries. We see how to do this in the next chapter.

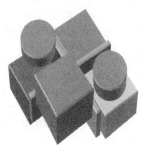

16
ADO and Data–Bound Controls

Introduction

If you want to have complete flexibility when developing your database applications you need to use do more of the work yourself, firstly to connect your data source to the application and then to connect data–bound components to fields in the data source. You will need to use SQL (Structured Query Language) to specify what data is to be read from the data source. The procedures which you have to follow are fairly straightforward, but if you are developing a simple application, it may be better to use the Visual Data Manager or the Data Form Wizard which will be faster and probably more bug–free than developing the application without these tools.

ActiveX data objects

Visual Basic supports three models for connecting to data sources; DAO (Data Access Objects), RDO (Remote Data Objects) and ADO (ActiveX Data Objects).

DAO was developed first and allowed Visual Basic applications to be connected to local Access and ODBC databases such as SQL Server using the Jet database engine. Jet is fast and efficient at accessing ISAM (Indexed Sequential Access Method) files, however when connecting to ODBC (Open Database Connectivity) databases the performance is poor. The file extension given to Access and Jet files is MDB.

RDO was designed to speed up access to ODBC databases, such as SQL Server or Oracle, but its performance when accessing ISAM files is not good.

The preferred data model for new Visual Basic applications is ADO rather than the previous two models, RDO and DAO. DAO and RDO are both being phased out and if you are starting a new database project in Visual Basic you should use ADO.

Database applications may need to connect to a wide variety of data sources: perhaps a simple text file, a local Access database or a distributed remote database. Typically most databases conform to the ODBC standard and can have their data read and manipulated using SQL, however a data source may be a non–relational database, an e–mail system or a simple text file. Microsoft provide a collection of COM (Component Object Model) interfaces, collectively called OLE DB, which provide a standard way of referencing a wide variety of data sources. ADO provides an applications programming interface between the application and OLE DB. The ADO model has significant benefits: in particular it does not occupy very much memory, it is fast when accessing a wide variety of data sources, it is flexible, and particularly useful for Visual Basic programmers is that it supports a wide range of events which allow you to follow every stage of the interaction between your application and the data source.

Data controls

There are three data controls which correspond to the DAO, RDO and ADO models. The DAO data control is one of the intrinsic controls on the standard Toolbox. We are going to use the ADO data control, which you will need to add to the Toolbox. Choose the **Projects | Components** menu option and select **Microsoft ADO Data Control 6.0**from the list of options.

The icon for the ADO data control is shown in figure 16.1.

Figure 16.1 *The ADO data control icon.*

ODBC providers

The ADO model provides a standard interface to your application (you can use the same interface with other languages such as Microsoft Visual C++ and even non–Microsoft languages such as Delphi), but for every type of data source there is a different service provider which handles the specific requirements of that data source while providing a standard programming interface to the application. The result of this is that you can use ADO to work with a wide variety of data sources without having to worry about their individual implementations. There are three native service providers for Jet, SQL Server and Oracle; others are available for different types of data source, but do not provide access which as extensive as for the native service providers.

ODBC is supplied with Visual Basic as well as many other Microsoft products and so it is extremely likely that it is already installed on your computer. If it is not you need to install it.

Creating a DSN

To connect a data source to your application you need to give that data source a DSN (Data Source Name). When you add the ADO data control to your application you specify this DSN to connect your application to the data source.

The simplest way to create a DSN is to run the Control Panel and to run the ODBC administrator using the icon shown in figure 16.2.

ODBC (32bit)

Figure 16.2 The ODBC administrator icon.

The ODBC Data Source Administrator is shown in figure 16.3. To add a data source click on the **Add** button.

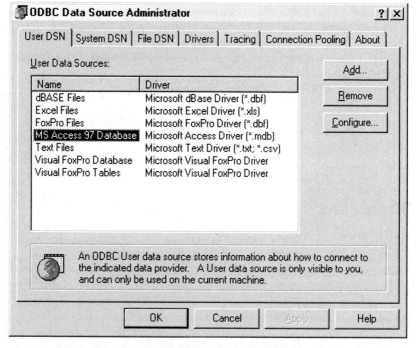

Figure 16.3 The ODBC Data Source Administrator.

The dialog shown in figure 16.4 asks you to select the type of driver you want to specify for the data source.

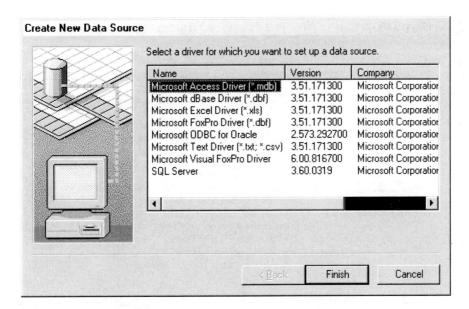

Figure 16.4 *Selecting a driver for the data source.*

In this case we want to specify **Microsoft Access Driver (*.mdb)** to allocate a DSN for the *Flights* Access database. Double click on this option to display the dialog shown in figure 16.5.

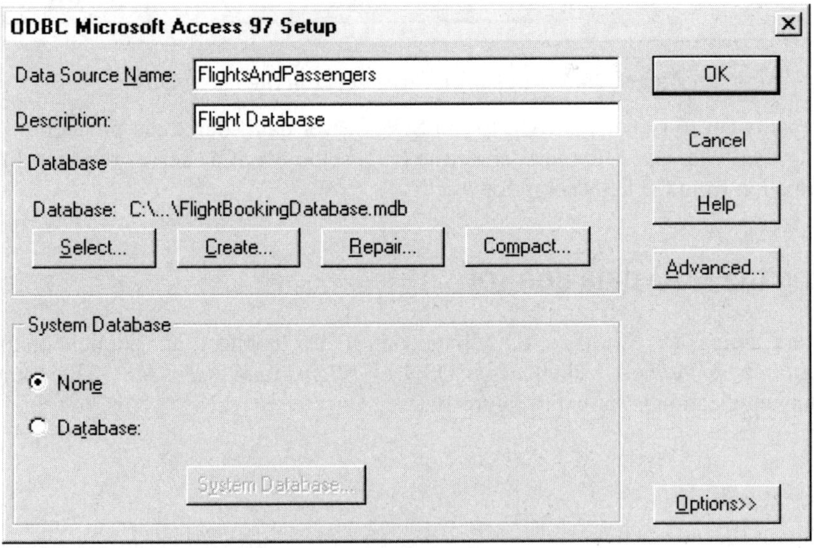

Figure 16.5 *Specifying the DSN.*

Click on the **Select** button to browse through your file system to find the database and specify the DSN and a description. In this case the DSN is *FlightsAndPassengers* and the description is *Flight Database*.

Click on **OK** to finish. Note that *FlightsAndPassengers* now appears in the list of user DSNs, as shown in figure 16.6.

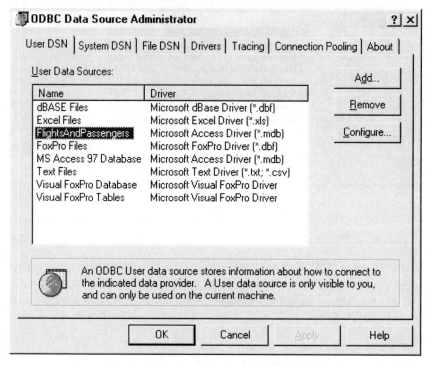

Figure 16.6 *FlightsAndPassengers in the list of DSNs.*

If you want to provide a DSN for an SQL Server data source the procedure is very similar, but there are differences since the DSN setup for SQL Server requires different information from the DSN setup for Access

Using the ADO data control

We are going to use the ADO data control to connect an application to the *FlightBookingDatabase* which has a DSN of *FlightsAndPassengers*. The completed running application is shown in figure 16.7.

Figure 16.7 *The completed application at run–time.*

* Start a new application using the **File | New Project** menu option and choose the **Standard EXE** option from the New Project dialog.
* If the ADO data control is not displayed in the Toolbox, add it using the **Project | Components** menu option and selecting **Microsoft ADO Data Control 6.0** from the **Controls** page.
* Add the ADO data Control to the application.
* Select the **ConnectionString** property. You can either type directly:

DSN = FlightsAndPassengers

or use the dialog as shown in figure 16.8.

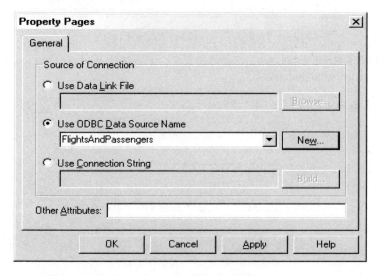

Figure 16.8 *Specifying the **ConnectionString** property.*

If you select the **Use ODBC Data Source Name** OptionButton and click on the down arrow or the list, you can select the DSN name without having to type it.

- Next we need to set up the **Recordset** property of the ADO data control, to specify the information we want to read from the record source. Select this property and either type the following SQL directly:

Select *FirstName, SecondName, Address, Origin,*
from *Passenger, Flight **where** Flight.FlightNo = Passenger.FlightNo*

or use the dialog to type it as shown in figure 16.9 to type the SQL.

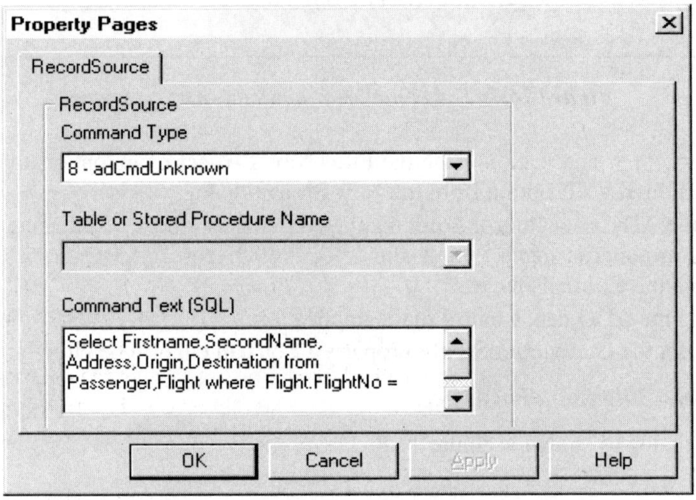

*Figure 16.9 Specifying the **Recordset** property.*

This completes the changes we need to make to the ADO data control to connect the data source to our application.

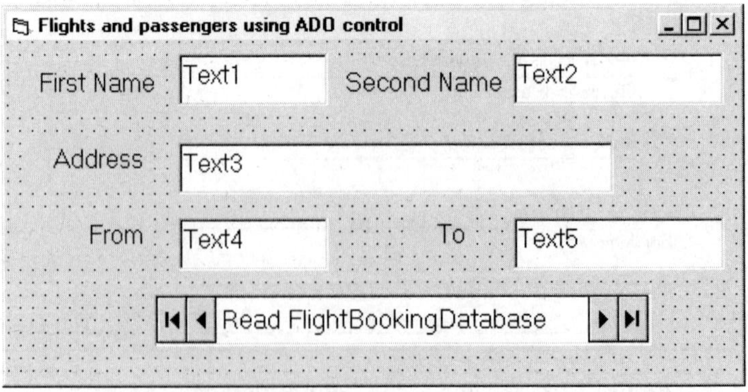

Figure 16.10 The completed application at design–time.

The next stage is to add a number of Label and TextBox controls, change the font size to 12 point and amend the **Caption** properties of the Form and ADO data control to create a form similar to that shown in figure 16.10.

At this stage the form is visually complete, but we have not yet established a link between fields in the record set and the TextBox controls. To complete the application:

- Change the **DataSource** property of all of the TextBox controls to the name of the ADO data control. If you are relying on Visual Basic default naming system this will be *Adodc1*.
- Change the **DataField** properties of *Text1*, *Text2*, *Text3*, *Text4*, and *Text5* to the names of the corresponding text fields in the data source, that is *FirstName*, *SecondName*, *Address*, *Origin*, *Destination*.

Properties of the ADO data control

To use the ADO data control fully, you need to be aware of its key properties.

Table 16.1 Key properties of the ADO data Control.

Property	Description
BOFAction	The **BOF** property is **True** when you have moved to the start of the record set. The **BOFAction** property can have either of two values: **rdMoveFirst** which keeps the first row as the current row and **rdBOF** which moves to the phantom record.
CacheSize	The number of records that are kept in the local memory.
CommandTimeout	Determines how long to wait for the execution of a command before abandoning it, if perhaps the network traffic is high. The default is 30 seconds. A value of zero means an indefinite wait.
EOFAction	The **EOF** property is **True** when you have moved to the end of the record set. The **EOFAction** property has three possible values: **rdMoveLast** keeps the last row as the current row; **rdEOF** moves to the phantom record; with **rdAddNew** a new record can be entered.
MaxRecords	Sets the maximum number or records which can be returned in a record set. Zero means there is no limit.
Mode	Controls the access of this connection and other connections to the data source. There are eight possible values specifying for example, a read–only connection.
Password	The password used to log on to the data source; if required.
RecordSource	The SQL statement, query or table which specifies the fields to be read from the data source.
UserName	The login identifier used to log on to the data source; it may not be required.

The application we have created works well, but we have relied on the default values of many of the properties of the ADO data control; however, there are some very useful facilities that it is worthwhile looking at in more detail as shown in table 16.1.

ADO data control events

We have seen in this application how to use the ADO data control to connect to a record source and how to use data–aware controls which display fields in the record set. One of the great features of Visual Basic is that you can achieve a lot without writing any Visual Basic code; however, if you want to use the full flexibility of the ADO model you do have to know about the events which occur when a database application runs, and how to respond to them. We are going to do this in the next chapter.

17

ADO Data Control Events

Introduction

To achieve complete flexibility in developing database applications we have to look at the events of the ADO data control and the properties and methods of the **Recordset** object. We can duplicate the functionality of the ADO data control by writing a few lines of Visual Basic code and add additional functionality to allow new records to be entered into the database and existing records to be amended or deleted.

The Recordset object

The **Recordset** object has a set of properties and methods (a method is an operation which is performed on a property). We are going to look at the methods initially and use them firstly to duplicate the functionality of the ADO data control and secondly to add some extra functionality, so that we can add, update and delete records.

The application we are going to look at displays the *Passenger* table and allows us to move through the **Recordset** and to update, delete and add new records. Note that this application does have an ADO data control which connects the application to the data source but it is invisible, that is its **Visible** property is **False**.

The running application we are going to develop is shown in figure 17.1.

To create this application, the first stage is to create the user interface: the completed application at design–time is shown in figure 17.2.

Change the **Name** properties of the TextBox controls to *TFirstName*, *TSecondName*, *TAddress*, *TFlightNo* and *TPassengerNo*, and the **Name** properties of the buttons to match the name of the **Caption** property which is displayed on the button face, that is *First*, *Previous*, *Next*, *Last*, *New*, *Update* and *Delete*.

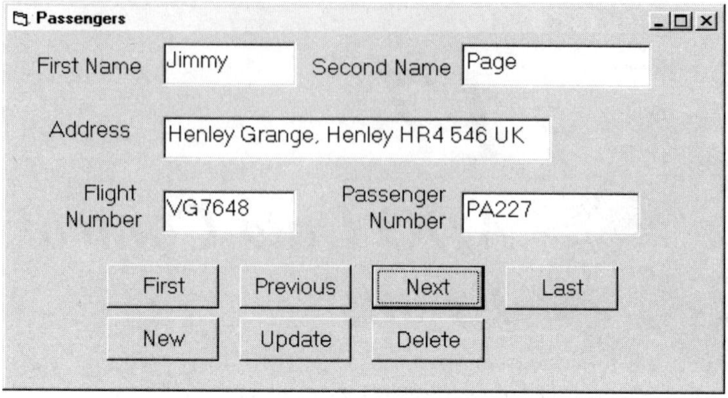

Figure 17.1 The completed application at run–time.

Ensure that the maximum number of permitted characters in each of the TextBox controls is the same as the size of the field which they are to display using the **MaxLength** property. Set this to 10 characters for *TFirstName*, 15 for *TSecondName*, 50 for *TAddress*, 6 for *TFlightNo* and 5 for *TPassengerNo*.

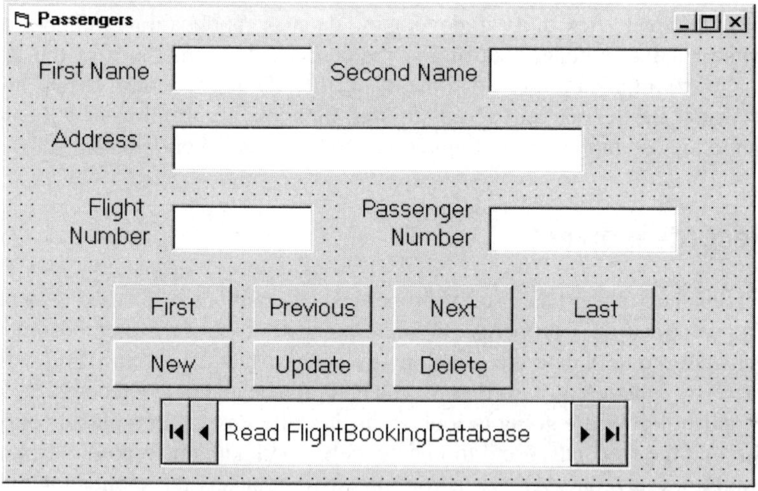

Figure 17.2 The completed application at design–time.

The ADO data control provides a connection between the data source and the application. To make this connection:

- Select the ADO data control.
- Select the **ConnectionString** property to display the Property Pages dialog as shown in figure 17.3. Select the **Use ODBC Data Source Name** option and select the *FlightsAndPassengers* DSN.

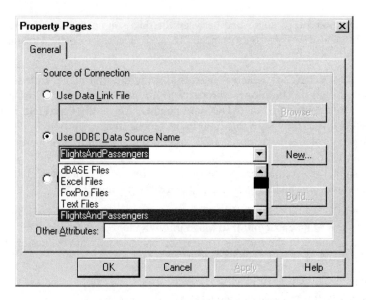

Figure 17.3 Selecting the data source.

Click on **OK** to show the dialog in figure 17.4.

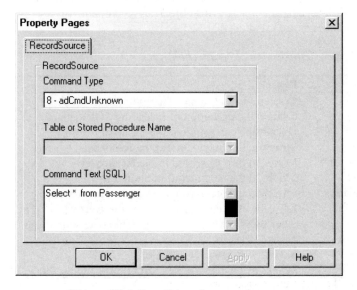

Figure 17.4 Specifying the record source.

Enter the following SQL into the **Command Text** TextBox:

Select * from *Passenger*

to read all of the fields in the *Passenger* table.

A link has now been established between the data source and the application. Each of the individual TextBox controls needs to be connected to a field from the record source.

- Select the TextBox which is used to display the first name, called *TFirstName* and change its **DataSource** property to *Adodc1*, to establish a link between the TextBox control and the **ADO data** control. Select the **DataField** property and assign this to the *FirstName* field in the record source.
- For each of the TextBox controls, assign the **DataSource** property of all these controls to *Adodc1*.
- Assign the **DataField** property to *SecondName* for the TextBox called *TSecondName* and so on for all of the TextBox controls.

If we run the application in its present form, none of the buttons will function, but you can use the ADO data control to move through the record source. The next stage is to add functionality to the buttons so that we can not only move through the record source, but also delete, update and add new records.

Methods of the Recordset object

To make our buttons active we need to write some Visual Basic code which manipulates the **Recordset** object. This object has a comprehensive set of methods; the most important ones are listed in table 17.1.

*Table 17.1 Key methods of the **Recordset** object.*

Property	Description
AddNew	Creates and adds a new record to the **Recordset**.
Cancel	Cancels the execution of a pending SQL statement or query.
Delete	Deletes the current record or group of records.
MoveFirst	Moves to the first record in the **Recordset**.
MoveLast	Moves to the last record in the **Recordset**.
MoveNext	Moves to the next record in the **Recordset**.
MovePrevious	Moves to the previous record in the **Recordset**.
ReQuery	Refreshes the entire contents of the **Recordset**. This is useful if other users have write access to the data source and the data may change.
Save	Saves the **Recordset** in a file.
Update	Saves any changes in the current record set to file.

Some of these methods are simpler to use than others, for example the **MoveFirst** method simply moves to the first record in the **Recordset**, however if you are using, for example, the **MoveNext** method you need to check that you are not already displaying the last record in the **Recordset**, and if you are, to take some alternative action.

When the button called *First* is clicked, the event procedure *First_Click* is called; we only need to add one line, which uses the **MoveFirst** method to move and display the first record in the **Recordset** as shown below:

```
Private Sub First_Click( )
    Adodc1.Recordset.MoveFirst
End Sub
```

Similarly to activate the button called *Last*:

```
Private Sub Last_Click( )
    Adodc1.Recordset.MoveLast
End Sub
```

The event procedure for the button which moves to the previous record is similar and uses the **MovePrevious** method. A second line is added to see if this moves to the phantom record at start of the **Recordset**, if it does the **MoveNext** method is executed to return to the first record in the **Recordset**. The effect of this is that if the first record is already displayed there is no change in the display. The event procedure is shown below:

```
Private Sub Previous_Click( )
    Adodc1.Recordset.MovePrevious
    If Adodc1.Recordset.BOF Then Adodc1.Recordset.MoveNext
End Sub
```

Similarly a check is made when the button called *Next* is clicked to see if the last record is already displayed:

```
Private Sub Next_Click( )
    Adodc1.Recordset.MoveNext
    If Adodc1.Recordset.EOF Then Adodc1.Recordset.MovePrevious
End Sub
```

The code for the *New* button consists of only one line. When the **AddNew** method is executed all of the TextBox controls are cleared, since the application moves to the phantom record at the end of the record set and all fields in this record are blank. You can type your own values. When you have done this, clicking on any other button will implicitly add the new record to the **Recordset**. You can explicitly add the new record by clicking on the *Update* button.

```
Private Sub New_Click( )
    Adodc1.Recordset.AddNew
End Sub
Private Sub Update_Click( )
    Adodc1.Recordset.Update
End Sub
```

The *Update* button has another function apart from saving new records to the data source: you can change any of the fields and then save these changes explicitly by clicking on this button, or implicitly by clicking on any of the buttons which move to a new record. It is important that you set the **MaxLength** property of the TextBox controls to the size of the fields which they are displaying since if you attempt to update the **Recordset** with a field which is too long (note that there may be trailing spaces in the TextBox controls) an error will result.

Another common problem when adding a new record is that if a mandatory field is left blank an error will be caused.

The *Delete* button uses the **Delete** method and then moves to display the next record. If the record deleted was the last, then the previous record is displayed:

> ***Private Sub*** *Delete_Click( )*
>   *Adodc1.Recordset.Delete*
>   *Adodc1.Recordset.MoveNext*
>   ***If** Adodc1.Recordset.EOF **Then** Adodc1.Recordset.MovePrevious*
> ***End Sub***

All of the buttons are now fully functioning although there is no error checking, for example to see if you are trying to add a blank record to the **Recordset**.

The final stage of the application is to set the **Visible** property of the ADO data control to **False**, so that it is invisible.

The **Recordset** object has a set of properties in addition to the methods which we have used; the most commonly–used properties are shown in table 17.2:

*Table 17.2 Key properties of the **Recordset** object.*

Property	Description
BOF	**True** if the cursor is pointing to the phantom record before the first record.
EditMode	One of four possible values: **adEditNone** indicates that no editing is in progress; **adEditInProgress**, the current row has been edited but not yet saved; **adEditAdd**, the **AddNew** method has been executed and a new row has been created which has not yet been added to the database; and **adEditDelete** which indicates that the current record has been deleted.
EOF	**True** if the cursor is pointing to the phantom record after the last record.
RecordCount	The number of records in the **Recordset**.

Events of the ADO data control

To get a fuller understanding of writing applications which use a data source we need to look at the events which can occur when data in a data–bound control changes.

The **WillChangeField** event occurs and the **WillChangeField** method is called for the ADO data control before a operation to change the value in one or more fields in the **Recordset**. The **FieldChangeComplete** method is called after the fields have been changed.

Similarly the **WillChangeRecord** method is called before one or more rows in the **Recordset** changes. The **RecordChangeComplete** method is called when the operation has happened.

The **WillMove** and **MoveComplete** methods are called before the current record changes and after the change has occurred.

If you want to check the sequence of these events when operations such as updating a record occur, add these methods to your application and include a single line in each which reports that the method has been called, for example in the **MoveComplete** method add the single line:

Debug.Print "MoveComplete"

The messages will be displayed in the Immediate window as shown in figure 17.5.

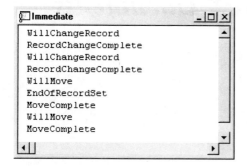

Figure 17.5 The Immediate window.

18

ActiveX Documents

Introduction

When you create an ActiveX document in Visual Basic you produce a Visual Basic application which is able to run within an ActiveX container, such as a suitable Web browser. The terminology ActiveX document is a confusing one, the analogy is often made between Microsoft Word document which can viewed within the Word application as well as other containers.

In this chapter we are going to see how to create an ActiveX document which can be viewed within Internet Explorer, and how to include hyperlinks.

Why use ActiveX documents?

If you want to create and distribute complex applications with hyperlinks, ActiveX documents have numerous advantages over other techniques:

- You can use all of the extensive development and debugging facilities of Visual Basic to develop applications, rather than learning other technologies such as HTML and Java.
- When placing controls on a Web page with HTML, many HTML editors do allow you to visually layout out your document. Visual Basic has excellent facilities for developing user interfaces.
- ActiveX documents can be run within a compatible browser, such as Internet Explorer, which is widely available.
- Hypertext links can be added to ActiveX documents.
- The asynchronous downloading of information is supported.
- You can use all Visual Basic controls except for the OLE container control.

The main negative aspect of using ActiveX technology is that is proprietary to Microsoft and may not be supported fully by non–Microsoft browsers, however Internet Explorer is available at very low cost or even free as a part of other applications.

Creating an ActiveX document

To start developing an ActiveX document application choose the **Projects | New Project** menu application and choose the **ActiveX Document EXE** icon (not the **ActiveX EXE** icon, which is the option to choose when you are creating a new ActiveX control).

Visual Basic creates a user document with a default name of *UserDocument1*. This document has a visual component on which you can add controls, and also a code component where you can write event procedures to handle the events from either the user document.

The application we are going to develop is shown in figure 18.1. It consists of a PictureBox control which contains six Shape controls which are shown as balls which bounce around the PictureBox control; when an edge is reached the balls bounce back into the PictureBox. The colour, initial position and speed of the balls is randomly chosen.

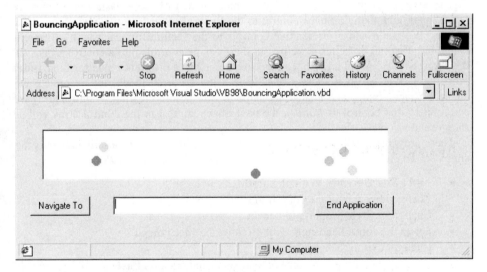

Figure 18.1 *The ActiveX document at run–time.*

Below the PictureBox is a TextBox control. You can type a URL into this TextBox and click on the *Navigate To* button to go to it. Clicking on the *End Application* button closes the ActiveX document and its container application. A menu item has also been added to the ActiveX document which is currently not visible.

To continue developing the application add a PictureBox, two CommandButtons and a TextBox to the user document to produce an appearance similar to that shown in figure 18.1. Change the names of the controls as follows:

- Project name to *Bouncing*.
- User document name to *BouncingApplication*.
- PictureBox name to *BouncingBalls*.
- Button names to *Navigate* and *CloseApp*.
- TextBox name to *URL*.

The next stage is to add the Shape controls which are shown as the balls in the PictureBox.

The Shape control

The icon for the Shape control, shown in figure 18.2, is straightforward to use and is useful for drawing simple shapes such as circles, squares, ovals, and round–cornered rectangles and squares.

     Figure 18.2 *The Shape control.*

The **Style** property of the control determines which of these basic five shapes are represented; add a single Shape control to the PictureBox and set the **Style** property to **Circle**. We could add a further five controls to the PictureBox, each with a different name, but it would be better if we placed these Shape controls into a control array. All the controls in a control array have the same name but a different value for their **Index** properties. We can then address the Shape using an array index, for example if we create a Shape control and change its name to *Ball* before creating a control array we can refer to that control as *Ball(0)*, the next Shape control in the control array will be *Ball(1)* and so on.

There are several ways to create a control array, but the way described here is the simplest. To create a control array of circular Shape controls called *Ball*:

- Add a Shape control to the PictureBox.
- Change the name of the control to *Ball*.
- Change its **Style** property to **Circle**.
- Select the control and right click to show the speed menu.
- Click on **Cut** in the speed menu.
- Right click to reveal the speed menu again and click on **Paste**.
- A dialog will be displayed as shown in figure 18.3, click on **Yes**.
- Repeatedly paste the control to create a total of six Shape controls, with index values from 0 to 5.

The user interface is complete, the next stage is to add the Visual Basic code.

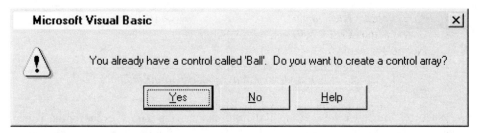

Figure 18.3 *Creating a control array.*

Creating an animation

To create the animated movement of the balls a Timer control is used. Add this control to the application; it does not matter where it is placed since it is invisible at run–time.

Set the **Enabled** property of the control to **True** and the **Interval** property at 100. This will trigger an event 10 times per second, which produces a fairly smooth movement.

The first stage in writing the Visual Basic code is to define two constants, *Diameter* and *NumberOfBalls* and two arrays, *x* and *y*, which will save the x and y distance by which the balls move every time a timer event occurs. The variables *x(0)*, *y(0)* give the change in position of the first element in the control array of shapes, *ball(0)* and so on:

```
' these variables are available throughout the whole module
Const Diameter = 200      ' size of balls
Const NumberOfBalls = 6
' the position of the balls
Private x(NumberOfBalls) As Single, y(NumberOfBalls) As Single
Option Explicit
```

When the application starts, the Initialise event occurs. In this event procedure we need to ensure that the balls are the same size, give them a random colour, random starting position and to allocate random values for the amount they will move in the x and y directions when the timer event occurs:

```
Private Sub UserDocument_Initialize( )
    Dim c As Integer
    For c = 0 To NumberOfBalls - 1
        Ball(c).Height = Diameter
        Ball(c).Width = Diameter
' choose a random colour for the interior and border of the balls
        Ball(c).BackColor = RGB(Rnd * 255, Rnd * 255, Rnd * 255)
        Ball(c).BorderColor = Ball(c).BackColor
' choose a random starting position
        Ball(c).Left = Rnd * BouncingBalls.Width - Diameter
        Ball(c).Top = Rnd * BouncingBalls.Height - Diameter
' choose a random value for the change in x and y when the timer expires
```

```
        x(c) = Rnd * 100
        y(c) = Rnd * 100
    Next c
' specify a valid URL for your system here
    URL.Text = "c:\books\vb\v6.0\activexdocument\index.htm"
End Sub
```

When the timer expires, every 100 milliseconds, the Timer event for the Timer control occurs. In this event we need to change the position of the balls in the x and y directions. If the vertical edge of the PictureBox control is reached the amount by which the ball moves in the x direction remains the same but its sign changes. This has the effect of making the ball seem to bounce off the PictureBox edge. The sign of the y change is reversed if either of the horizontal edges is reached:

```
Private Sub Timer1_Timer( )
    Dim c As Integer
' change the balls position
' if the edge of the container is reached reverse the direction
    For c = 0 To NumberOfBalls - 1
        Ball(c).Left = Ball(c).Left + x(c)
        Ball(c).Top = Ball(c).Top + y(c)
        If Ball(c).Left >= BouncingBalls.Width - Ball(c).Width Or _
                    Ball(c).Left <= 0 Then x(c) = 0 - x(c)
        If Ball(c).Top >= BouncingBalls.Height - Ball(c).Height Or _
                    Ball(c).Top <= 0 Then y(c)= 0 - y(c)
    Next c
End Sub
```

The last two event procedures we need to write are for the two buttons. When the *CloseApp* button is clicked the application is ended:

```
Private Sub CloseApp_Click( )
    End ' end the application
End Sub
```

When the *Navigate* button is clicked a hypertext link to the specified URL is carried out. The URL is typed into the TextBox control called *URL*.

```
Private Sub Navigate_Click( )
    Hyperlink.NavigateTo URL.Text        ' go to specified URL
End Sub
```

If you want you can create your own HTML document, and put in a link back to the ActiveX document in the same way in which you would add a hypertext link to another HTML document.

Adding forms and menus to ActiveX documents

You can add forms and menus to ActiveX documents in the same way they are added to standard Visual Basic applications. The difference in the way in which menu items are handled is that they are not displayed on the ActiveX document itself, but added to the menu system of the container application.

Even if you do not want to add a menu system to your ActiveX document it is always advisable to add an about box, even if is it only so that you know which version of the application is being used.

To add an about box, click on the **Project | Add Form** menu item. Display the **New** page and select the **About Dialog** icon. You can edit the dialog in the same way as for a standard Visual Basic application to create a dialog similar to the one shown in figure 18.4.

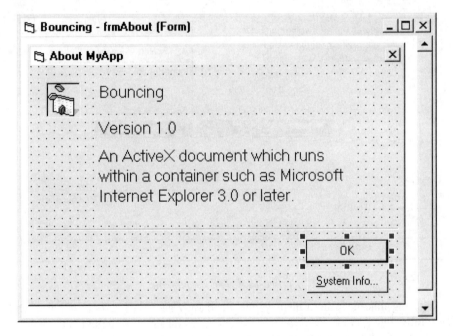

Figure 18.4 *The about dialog.*

To add a menu:

- Run the **Menu Editor** by selecting the **Tools | Menu Editor** menu option or by clicking on the icon on the tool bar.
- Add a menu item with a caption of *&Help* and a name of *mnuHelp*.
- Add a second menu item with a caption of *About Bouncing* and a name of *mnuAboutBouncing*.
- Indent the second item so that it is one level below the first item.
- Add the event procedure for the About Bouncing menu item so that it displays the about box, which has been left with the default name of *frmAbout*.

The event procedure is shown below:

Private Sub *mnuAboutBouncing_Click( )*
   *frmAbout.***Show**   *'display the about box*
End Sub

If you are unclear about how to use the **Menu Editor** it is covered in detail in chapter 7.

You will not see a menu at the top of the user document at design–time or run–time, but if you run the application and click on the Help menu, you will see a menu option has been added, *BouncingApplication Help*, which has a single sub–menu option *About Bouncing*, as shown in figure 18.4.

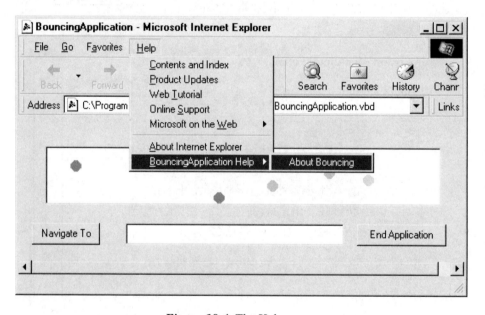

Figure 18.4 *The Help menu.*

Selecting this menu item displays the standard Visual Basic About window, which has a fully–function *System Info* button which gives information about the hardware and software of the host computer.

ActiveX containers

One of the difficulties with creating an ActiveX document is that you are not sure what container will be used to view it. This is a hazard which it is not possible to overcome, but at least you can check to see a browser is being used to open the document using the **TypeName** method. This method returns a string indicating the type of an object. The Show event occurs when an ActiveX document is placed on a container and therefore this is the best place to check to see if the container is appropriate, by looking at the **Parent** property of the user document. If the string returned is either *IWebBrowser* or

IWebBrowser2, then the container is a suitable web browser. You can check to see if either of these strings is returned. If they are not then you can display a warning dialog as shown in figure 18.6 and end the application.

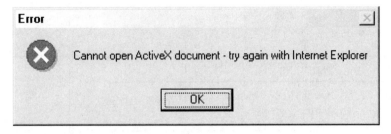

Figure 18.6 *Action on finding an invalid container.*

The event procedure for the Show event is shown below:

```
Private Sub UserDocument_Show( )
    Dim Container As String
    Container = TypeName(UserDocument.Parent)
    If Container <> "IWebBrowser" And Container <> "IWebBrowser2" Then
        MsgBox "Cannot open ActiveX document - " & _
            "try again with Internet Explorer", vbCritical, "Error"
        End
    End If
End Sub
```

Other possible strings which can be returned by **TypeName** are *Section* and *Window* if the application is opened by Microsoft Binder or if the window is created by the *CreateToolWindow* function in the Visual Basic IDE.

The ActiveX document Viewport

Since an ActiveX document is not a stand–alone application, but can only be viewed within a container, it is possible that all of the document will not be visible as shown in figure 18.7. If this is the case horizontal and vertical scrollbars are added as required. You can find out the size of the container by using the **ViewPointWidth** and **ViewPointHeight** properties of the **UserDocument**.

The **ViewPortLeft** and **ViewPortTop** properties give the distances from the left and top edges of the ActiveX document to the left and top edges of the container. The default when the ActiveX document is loaded into the container is that **ViewPortLeft** and **ViewPortTop** will both be zero, which is the case in figure 18.7. As you move around the document using the scrollbars these values change.

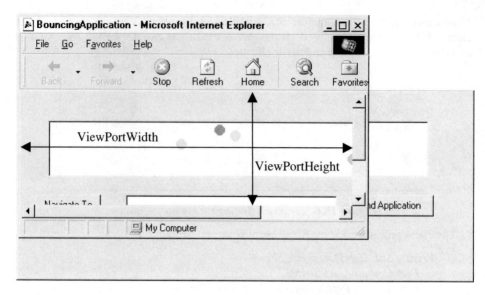

Figure 18.7 *The Viewport.*

If the ActiveX document is smaller than the container, the document is displayed in the top left corner of the document (with **ViewPortLeft** and **ViewPortTop** both zero) and the surrounding area outside the document is the document's background colour.

The ActiveX document Migration Wizard

The ActiveX document Migration Wizard converts existing forms into ActiveX documents. It is fairly limited, but can be a useful tool. While it converts forms into ActiveX documents it does not change the type of your application to an ActiveX document application. The wizard carries out the following actions:

- Converts forms into user documents.
- Menu items are added to the menu of the container, but only the Help menu is merged with the container menu. This means that if you have a menu item called *File* in the form you are converting, this will appear in addition to the *File* menu in the container, so that there will be two *File* menu headings.
- Copies all controls to the user documents. The positions and properties of the controls are unchanged.
- Converts all event handlers into ActiveX document event handlers and copies them to the ActiveX document.

The wizard will comment out **Show**, **Hide** and **End** statements if you request it, but you may get compiler errors if your form contains any code which is not compatible with an ActiveX document, for example OLE embedding.

The wizard can be run from the **Add–Ins | ActiveX Document Migration Wizard** menu option. If this option is not available on your menu system select the **Add–Ins | Add–In Manager** and specify that you want to include the wizard.

An introductory dialog is displayed first giving some background information on the wizard. You can click on a CheckBox so that this dialog is not shown when the wizard is next run. The next dialog, shown in figure 18.8, lists the forms in the project and allows you to select the ones you wish to convert to ActiveX documents.

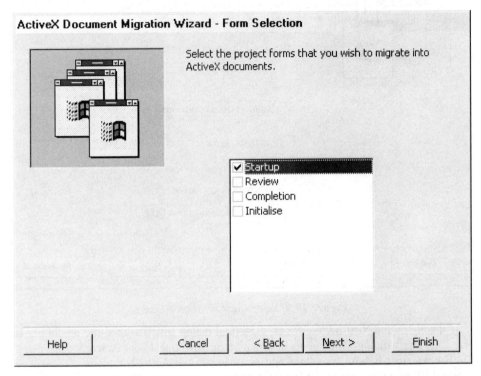

ActiveX Document Migration Wizard - Form Selection

Select the project forms that you wish to migrate into ActiveX documents.

- ☑ Startup
- ☐ Review
- ☐ Completion
- ☐ Initialise

| Help | Cancel | < Back | Next > | Finish |

Figure 18.8 Selecting forms to migrate.

The options dialog shown in figure 18.9 offers the option of commenting out invalid code; in practice it actually comments statements which include the **Show**, and **Hide** methods and the **Unload** and **End** statements.

You can remove the original forms from the project, but they are not deleted and still remain on disk.

If the current project is a standard EXE or ActiveX Control project you must convert it to either an ActiveX EXE project or an ActiveX DLL project. If you want to create an ActiveX document and not a DLL choose the default first option.

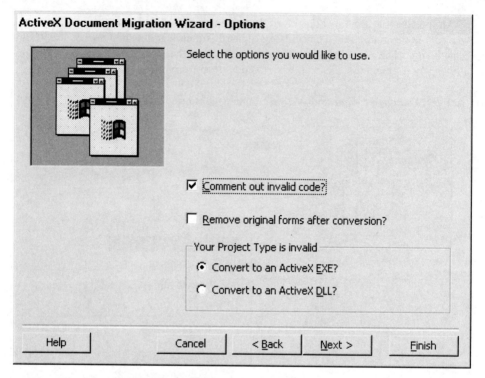

Figure 18.9 *Selecting migration options.*

Clicking on the Next button displays the final dialog which asks if you would like to see a summary dialog which gives information on how to test your ActiveX document.

The wizard has now completed and you can run the ActiveX documents you have created. While there are many limitations in the capabilities of this wizard, it can be a useful tool for converting simple applications into ActiveX documents.

Index